MAKE MONEY BLOGGING

....Strategies To Earn Passive Income

PAUL D. KINGS

ISBN: 9781723929137

CONTENTS

INTRODUCTION

Thank you for downloading this fantastic guide—**"Make Money Blogging - Strategies to Earn Passive Income."**

This ebook is written for those new to blogging and want to earn passive income.

Why you should buy this book:

1. It combines instruction on how to earn passive income through blogging.

2. It shows you how to build your blog and exceptional skills to enable you to create your content and products.

3. It helps you to see beyond the concept of writing blog for free and consumption and looks at ways you can exploit the fantastic skills and passion you've got to earn money through blogging. This and many more are embedded inside this guide, and you will never regret buying this book.

I hope you enjoy the book and please do leave a review. Best

Paul D. Kings

Blogging is a brilliant way to get out in the online world and an excellent way to start getting recognition as an expert in your chosen field. Over 175,000 people start a new blog every single day, so you want to start out with the right foot forward to, you know, stay ahead of 'the pack.'

Blogging can be an enjoyable hobby. You get to write about your favorite topics and spark conversation with other bloggers. Most people blog to make money. While this is difficult to achieve, it can be done with the right amount of work. Before you worry about making money with your blog, you have to set it up first.

There are numerous ways you can make money with your blog. You can place ads from Google or Bidvertiser on your blog. They will pay you each time a visitor clicks on one of their ads. You can also get set up with affiliate sites. These work well with blogs and pay well. Blogging for money requires a lot of patience and tweaking. To make money blogging, you will need to have sufficient traffic.

Updating your blog will require a commitment from you. You'll need to establish a regular time to search for and write about fresh news and get it posted. There'll be times when not much has happened, and there'll be times when you can't type fast enough.

But two or three times a week are not too many to post something new. Even if it's only to tell your readers that not much has been going on, share a few thoughts, and tell your readers when to make an appearance next. Your audience will keep coming back as long as they know you are.

Keep your blog as simple as you can, without sounding like you don't have a complete grasp of your subject. You want to appeal to as many people as possible, and nothing will drive those newly interested in a subject away faster than lots of technical jargon and statistics. You can provide complex information, as long as you make an effort to put it in user-friendly terms.

Find a memorable name for your blog, and use your blog editing feature to post it in large, bold-face type. "My Hiking Blog" will probably sound interesting only to Mom and Dad and only because you never write or call them while you're out adventuring. "Climbing through the Clouds" will appeal to those who either tackle the high places of the Earth or want to.

Every so often, say, at the end of each month, archive your existing blog posts. Your blog editor will let you do this in a less than a minute. The entries will still be available for new blog readers who want to catch up, or those who wish to reference your earlier writings. And list keywords for your archived work so that new traffic will be able to find its way to you.

Finally, make sure your blog is professionally presented. You have a spell checker, so use it. Proof-read your copy and correct any grammar or punctuation errors before you post your work. If you're not sure whether you are using a word correctly, get help from an online dictionary. Respect your readers as intelligent, well-informed people who could just as easily spend their time elsewhere.

These suggestions may make your entry into the world of blogging more successful, but it's up to you to commit to building and keeping an audience.

Let's Get Started!

CHAPTER 1

MAKE MONEY BLOGGING

A Means to Make Money Blogging for Beginners?

Have you been wondering the best way to make money blogging for beginners? You might have possibly heard people can make an excellent living online, blogging straight from their residence.

When you create a blog, you're doing two basic things:

❖ You are defining a voice with the excellent content material.
❖ You are building yourself a target market.
❖ You will find several approaches to choose from blog setup and learning.

First of all, you can use the public free of charge hosted blogging platforms available through Blogger.com and WordPress.com. These are generally straightforward, no-frills solutions which merely began with a login registration. The service will host your blog on his or her server. You can start to write your posts as soon as your blogging platform is set up. You can add a great deal more flexibility to your blog when you host your blog. It will demand some additional actions.

Initially, you will purchase hosting by one of the reputable providers. It simply means you rent some space on a server to create your blog and make it accessible to the internet. You might start with a simple hosting package for $50 or less for your first year which normally jumps up to about $100 per year.

When Do You Start The Process?

If you are trying to make money online, then monetizing your blog is inevitable. The question is when starting a blog when does the money making process begin? When is the proper time for a blogger to start to make money from blogging?

There are two lines of thought or approaches, as when to monetize your blog. There are those who believe you should wait until you have a large audience or readership before trying to make any money. Then there are those who believe in monetizing your blog from the start.

Let's take a look at both approaches and see what method will best work for you and your blog.

❖ The Monetize Later Approach

The primary concern of starting a blog is to provide valuable content and to drive traffic to your blog. Bloggers who take this approach feel that they can build a larger audience by not including ads or attempt to make money blogging from the very start. Building traffic by providing valuable content is the key. With this approach the reader's focus is entirely on the content rather than the ads, resulting in creating an audience faster.

Those who use the monetize later approach feel that new blogs are unlikely to make any significant amount of money on ads and affiliate programs without having an established reader base. In other words, if you aren't going to make any money, whatever ads you may have will not be beneficial to your blog and may result in losing your audience. Blog readers want to read your blog; they don't want to click on advertisements. So to make money blogging, focus on building content, to write good posts, build trust with your readers then start to filter in your process to generate income with your blog.

❖ The Monetize Now Approach

Some bloggers choose to monetize their blog from the very start. They want to make money from blogging from the very beginning. They feel that readers expect to see some ads when they visit any blog. One of the benefits to monetize your blog at the very beginning is that it will give you more time to learn about your market.

By placing ads early, you can learn what your readers are responding to: what types of ads are working well and where is the best placement for your ads. It makes the design of your blog more accessible. In other words, you won't have to redesign your blog when you start monetizing later. As you begin to see how your blog is performing, the process of adding more ads will be more straightforward.

Keep ads to a minimum. A good tip when starting a blog is to avoid the use of pop-up or pop-down and flashing ads on your blog. These ads are very annoying and may lead to your visitor quickly leaving your blog site.

You may be able to make some money earlier. It might not be a lot, but it can cover some of your operating costs. Making a little money may encourage you to bigger and better things.

Is It Really Possible?

Not only is it possible, but it can be fun as well. If you want to build an online business to make money, there are other ways that you could do it, but blogging is probably the most inexpensive. Some people will argue that it is the most fun also.

When you are trying to decide on a topic to blog about, think about what you are naturally interested in. Don't pick an issue just because it will make you money. That is a consideration, but you want this to be something you enjoy doing also. Because you will be doing this after you get home from work, and you want to look forward to it, not view as another chore you have to do. If you enjoy it, you will continue to do it and not come up with excuses why you can't.

Now one thing to keep in mind is that there is work involved. You are not going to throw a blog up today, and be making 4 figures a month in 30 days.

That has happened, but it is rare. You will have to spend time building your blog into a trusted source of information. You will be building the number of visitors to your blog slowly at first, but as time goes by your traffic will gain momentum. It could take a few months, or it could take a couple of years, it all depends on you.

You need to become a student of blogging. You should study what other bloggers are doing, not just any bloggers, but those who are making money. You can get a right amount of information by searching online and looking for free information. You will speed up your success along though if you find some bloggers you can get training from.

Pro Blogging Basics

It is not uncommon for individuals to begin their lives as a blogger with the idea that they can become a pro blogger, and start blogging for dollars. The biggest downfall to this mentality is becoming a pro blogger, and to make money blogging is a process that takes time and effort, and will not happen overnight.

This results in a lot of failed blogs on the internet abandoned to collect the proverbial internet dust, and in my mind is a sad state to leave one's hopes and dreams.

Blogging for dollars is not difficult. But many people have very high expectations. And very low thresh hold for failure. If your primary objective when starting your first blog is to make money blogging, then you will fail. In many cases it takes month, if not years for your blog to have enough content to even generate any interest. It is human nature always to want more, and if your blog cannot support our need, we will move on.

So, how do you start blogging for dollars?

You start with the basics. You start with a concept or idea for a blog in a niche market that interests you enough for you to be able to generate daily content about the niche you select. You can do this by merely thinking of things that occupy your spare time. Hobbies, sports, interests, it can almost be anything you can think of. The primary objective is to have a topic you will not quickly lose interest in because in the beginning the dollars will not be rolling in, in fact, if cents are turning in you are ahead of many beginner bloggers out there.

But there is more to a topic than just finding your enjoyment. It is critical to see a topic that is not already overpopulated on the Internet. There are several things you can do to check this. After establishing your topic, search for it using Google, and see how many results you get. If you have a topic that generates under 100,000 web page results, you may have a chance with that topic, some topics may turn back millions upon millions of results, and although this is not a make or break step, it is essential to know how heavy your competition is.

The real key to this search is to determine the Page rank of the top ten websites within your topic; this will help you identify if you will be able to break into the first page of the search engine results. You can find out page rank by downloading Google's toolbar.

There are other tools though, so choose the one you are comfortable with. The critical point to remember is, any site with a page rank of 4 will be tough for you to compete with. If the first page is loaded with PR 4's and higher, you may want to refine your keyword a bit to see if you can find a more accessible market.

A simple way to refine your primary niche or Keyword is by using Google's AdWords Keyword Tool; this tool will give you the search totals for your chosen keyword, along with suggested keywords that would fall within your niche.

Once you have established your niche market, it is essential to stay on topic. Blog daily about your niche, offering useful information that leaves a reader wanting more. It is key to generating traffic, and traffic is the key to blogging for dollars.

Once you have established a writing pattern, and are writing consistent content. Your next responsibility as a new and budding pro blogger, to read other blogs within your niche market and from this, you can gather useful information on what others within your market are talking about. On top of that, it offers you the chance to comment on others blogs.

Blog commenting is critical. This not only generates awareness or you and your blog, but it also opens up a possible business relationship with the other blogger. As long as your comment is insightful and not viewed as spam, there is a chance that a conversation can be struck up between you and the other blogger. It opens the door for link exchanging and guest blogging, both of which offer you the chance for more readers.

Now that you are writing consistent content, and you are commenting and networking with other bloggers within your niche marketing, the next step to blogging for dollars is backlinks. Building backlinks will be the primary concern for you in establishing reliable and consistent page views. Backlinks, using your primary keywords will attract search engine spiders. Increasing the number of times your blog is indexed and also growing your Page ranking. The goal is to generate enough backlinks to be seen on the first page of any search engine for your specific keywords.

Blogging In Your Spare Time

There are thousands of ways to make money online, but if you are more of the creative type or you have an exciting or witty outlook on life, you might want to consider starting your blog. Blogging is easy. It's free and best of all you can make money with little to no additional effort.

The internet provides businesses with a strong global marketplace of potential consumers. Companies are always looking for new and more creative marketing outlets, and blogs offer retailers with convenient access to their target market. Companies buy advertising space on people's blogs every day, and many bloggers have been able to turn a fun hobby into a lucrative career.

Advertising space on blogs works just like advertising on TV. The more popular, prime-time shows sell their commercial space at a higher rate because they are giving advertisers access to a broader audience. So, the more people and readership your blog attract the more valuable advertising space on your blog becomes. So basically you need to create exciting content that appeals to a large group of people.

If you are starting your blog to make a profit, you will want to investigate what blogs are already out there and determine how you can make yours stand out above the rest. Find a unique angle utilizing your skills, interests, and background. You can be creative, be authentic. Blogs that are fake or over commercialized lack mass appeal.

3 Productive Activities That Help You Make Money Blogging

With so many things to do, you can easily get overwhelmed. Although they make it seem so simple, the devil is always in the detail. Fortunately, you can focus on the most important things and still multiply your income. Figuring out which tasks are essential can be difficult. Based on years of my experience, here they are.

1. Persuade

You need to persuade in everything that you do. You want readers to peruse your blog content. For that, you write magnetic headlines or titles. Make the title irresistible so they can't help but click and read the rest of the article. When you need them to subscribe to your RSS feed, you sell them the benefits of doing so. The same thing applies to the buying decision. You want to persuade them, so they feel good about buying.

If you decide to be an affiliate and sell other people's product, you also need to persuade people to the click and take a look at what you recommend. This technique is called pre-selling. You want to learn how to make people take action.

It doesn't have to be a bad thing as long as the actions they take are going to move them at least one step closer to their goal.

2. Network

Blogging is a communication and interaction tool. You can't grow your blog if you don't network with other blogs. Bloggers will link to other people if they already know him/her. At least it is more likely for them to do so. They also will pay more attention if you already cultivate the relationship with them.

Talking about the relationship, you also need to do that with your audience. Don't leave them cold. They don't like that. Especially nowadays, they expect to be a part of the community by participating actively. That's why they try to be active in blog comments. So talk to them.

3. Optimizing

You need to keep finding things that you can maximize to get better results. Perhaps you should ask the readers to subscribe to your RSS feed if they see your blog post interesting.

You should also test different spots to place ads. If you use AdSense, you should find ways to get the most clicks by examining shapes and colors too.

By continually optimize your blog; you will increase your income from existing traffic. When you grow your blog, you will be able to make more money with less traffic compared to other blogs which fail to optimize.

CHAPTER 2

FINDING AUTHENTIC WAYS OF MAKING MONEY ON THE INTERNET

Interesting Writing Is Interesting Reading

The explosion of online content that has occurred over the last decade has opened up so many opportunities to those who take advantage of them. With broadband internet, wireless technology and mobile computing, there have never been more ways to make money on the internet.

For those who wish to make money blogging, this chapter will explore one of the critical factors for your success. The first key to really turning your blog into a traffic and revenue generator is to make it interesting. That's the foundation of how to make money blogging: if your writing is exciting and captivates your audience, it will begin to generate income.

Sounds so simple, right? Well, the truth is that while exciting writing is critical to your efforts to make money blogging, it is a bit more difficult than it sounds. It has to be, or else everyone would be a millionaire writing about anything, wouldn't' they?

So precisely what does it mean, "Interesting writing is interesting reading?" Well, there are three essentials to making your blog interesting.

Essential #1 - Your blog Must be Interesting to you

Perhaps the crucial aspect of how exciting writing can help you make money blogging is the idea that what you write about should be fascinating to you. The best writers write about what they love. And the best writing is born of love and excitement about something.

So when you choose to create a blog, pick a general topic that is something about which you're passionate. If you are interested in writing about politics, and politics is something you find fascinating, you are much more likely to convey that excitement to your reader and get them excited about it too.

Essential #2 - Write for people

We won't go into how good a writer you may or may not be. Quantifying anyway is hard. And besides, even if you aren't excellent, over time, with practice, you'll get better. Especially if you follow essential #1. However, no one will ever make money blogging by merely spinning somebody else's work, or paying a non-native writer to try and write in your language or to hope Google ranks your blog.

Write your blog. Take the time to think it through, spell check it, proofread it and take it seriously. Yes, you want to optimize the blog entries for search results, but don't do so naturally. If your readers can't understand or are annoyed by your writing, no one will participate or refer anyone else. And if it's crap writing, you'll get crap results from Google, Yahoo and Bing.

Essential #3 - Original Work

It is a short but essential for your goal to make money blogging. DO NOT copy others' work. Don't spin articles, don't cut corners. Original content carries so much more weight because it comes from the heart, the head and conveys your sincere effort and desire to please the readers.

The trick to making money blogging is to put forth a real effort. Exciting writing comes from a real solid effort. When you do the work, you'll see the results. It can't be so straightforward to make money blogging, or everyone would do it, as mentioned above.

When you take the time to pick a topic that is interesting to you, write blog entries that are compelling and meant to stimulate the reader and print them from scratch, you'll not only get more traffic and more readers, and you'll create a solid foundation on which a thriving income can be established.

Get Personal And The Profits Will Roll In

The business of blogging can be advantageous and profitable with the right mindset.

You CAN make money by writing your blog. But if you start blogging with the primary goal to make money, you've already slowed your success down. Your goal, as a blogger, is to create a following... a community of people who want be like you, read what you have to say and are compelled to come back to your blog day after day.

Why is this important?

People visit and read content from YOU. They're not visiting your site for the site... and they certainly don't visit to be sold. People buy from people, not from stores.

Oprah has a following colossal right? She's so well respected by her community that all she has to do is say "buy this shirt" and her followers will do just that. They trust her. They love her. She is a rockstar for them. That is what you want to be for your blog. The rockstar. The person, your readers, respect, like and follow. When you have this community, they will trust you, and they will buy from you.

So, how do you become a rockstar?

Well, you're not going to start a band. Well.... You need to get personal. Write your content with honesty and sincerity. Write it with personal stories. Share. Be transparent. And of course, provide valuable content that is compelling. When you do this, you begin to build a relationship with your readers... and this builds trust. When they trust you, they will do whatever you tell them to do.

If you are a blogger, building trust will go a long way to strengthening your readership and for readers to believe in what you say. It will only help your customer base grow, your traffic to your blog to increase and honestly... you will enjoy your business so much more!

By being personal and honest with your readers, they will not feel scammed. No one likes to get pulled in by content that thought would be valuable only to be hit left and right with cold product offers and hard sales. Yuck. No thank you.

You CAN make money blogging... while staying in honest and personal. It starts with you providing content that will genuinely help your readers solve a problem... a common problem among your community.

When your content is targeted specifically to your community and niche... and you tell them about a product or service honestly... share a personal story along with it... you will realize success beyond your wildest dreams.

Top Reasons Why You Should Start A Blog

Blogging is here to stay. One is hard-pressed in this day and age to find anyone under the age of 30 who doesn't know what a blog is. Anyone can maintain a blog. There aren't any rules when it comes to blogging other than to have the ability to produce original content. It's not necessary to be witty or satirical although it is helpful.

If you have been thinking about starting a blog of your own, or wondering what the blog buzz is all about, then this is for you. Outlined below are 10 reasons why YOU should start a blog.

1. Blogging is fun.

There hundreds of sites dedicated to hosting blogs. Most, if not all, have templates and add-ons that allow you to customize your blog. You will have your personalized corner of the web in no time.

2. Blogging is therapeutic.

... mainly if you use your blog for venting your frustrations about anything. After a long, hard day at work or play, a blog is a beautiful place to unwind and regain your focus. Most blogging platforms allow commenting, and you can often gain useful insight from commentators offering constructive thoughts. Your blog is an unconditional listener.

3. Blogging is a great way to share your voice.

If you are an individual who is opinionated by nature or passionate about a particular topic, your blog is an open forum waiting for your views. You can share your thoughts with the world no matter what they are. Blogging will offer you the chance to meet like-minded people and host friendly debates with opposing views.

4. Blogging is the easiest and cheapest way to self-publish.

There is a myriad of self-publishers who will charge an arm and a leg to put your name in print. Then you are still left to market your work yourself. If you are going to promote yourself, you might as well do it via blogging and save yourself a small fortune in printing costs. Not to mention there is enormous potential to reach a wider audience because you have the Wide World Web at your fingertips.

5. Blogging is an excellent networking resource.

Once you have created your blog and begun to post regularly, it's time to network and reach a broader audience.

The internet has dozens of places dedicated solely to bloggers for URL submission, RSS feed distribution, and blogging communities to join. You will never want for new sites and ways to promote your blog.

6. Blogging allows you to focus on a targeted audience.

When you are considering blogging for the first time, you should think about who you want your audience to be. Are you just writing a running record of your life? Are you trying to make a point? Perhaps you are writing to help and inspire others. It's a good idea to pick a particular niche and stick to it. It will help with networking and also promoting.

7. Blogging provides a platform for self-education.

A blog is a great place to document the experience. Whether you are trying out a new kind of skin cream or testing a new affiliate marketing client, blogging gives you the opportunity to learn from your experiences as well as share those experiences with others.

Allowing others to gain from your experiences can earn an excellent reputation in the Blogosphere.

8. Blogging can make you money.

It's not a secret that maintaining a blog can make you money. There are thousands of resources online that will give you the necessary tools you need to start earning from your writing. You can monetize your blog using one or more of several methods such as pay-per-click advertising, affiliate programs, pay-per-post, paid reviews, etc. It is a lot easier and more possible than it may sound, and anyone can do it.

9. Blogging can be used to communicate with friends and family.

If you have a lot of friends and family members who all want to know what's going on in your life, there is no better way to reach an audience than by blogging about your days. You can keep family and friends abreast of events, life changes, and anything else worthy of note. It's the absolute perfect way to keep an informed and supportive group close even when miles may separate you.

10. Blogging makes for an entertaining hobby.

Whether you are blogging for your hobby or blogging about a hobby, writing for yourself and others is entertaining. You can be yourself and write about anything you desire. The more your blog fulfills the purpose you have in mind when you start it, the more entertaining it will be for you.

Will Google AdSense Help You Make Money Blogging?

Without a doubt, Google is one of the most popular search engines on the Internet. They also have a well-liked marketing program known as Google AdSense.

❖ Try it out to help monetize your blog.

Advertising scares some people. They are not into direct advertising and things like that. Do you fall into this category? If so, don't worry, there is a solution.

Google AdSense makes it uncomplicated for people with no marketing skills or a worry of marketing to monetize their websites or blogs.

❖ The Ins and Outs

Google AdSense, in essence, places targeted ads on your blog. You fill out the re☐uired data on their site when you sign up for a free account & if your blog is about golf, for instance, your ads will revolve around that subject matter also.

Google has many features to help content publishers - that's you. If you have a search facility on your blog, you can use AdSense to earn money from readers clicking on the search results from your site and also the Web.

The most widespread use of this advertising program is for content. They will place ads on your blog that will get noticed. You can arrange these ads where you deem they will be best received by your readers.

Once you are accepted by the program and commence your account, you can get rolling immediately. Be sure to peruse all the policies and criteria before proceeding, so you don't fall foul of the Google gods.

Furthermore, your money is deposited right away. You receive a fee each time someone clicks on those ads. C'Mon! You've just made your first step towards making money.

Best of all, you don't have to take care of those ads. You can keep on blogging and hit upon other ways to monetize your blog even though the ads do their thing without you. It is every non-advertiser's Utopia.

❖ Try Google AdSense on All of Your Blogs.

If You Have More Than One Blog Sign up to Monetize all of them. You could place ads on every blog you have that are tailored to your pre-re ☐uisite for that blog.

Google offers tools to help you handle your money and each account you have with them. If you choose to evolve your blogs into a business, you can use Google's Ad Manager to keep tabs on your cash and the ads that are bringing it in.

When you are ready, you can transfer up to other advertising apparatus like AdWords. At this point, you can advertise on search engine pages to amplify your visibility and then initiate your ads.

Scared it takes too much effort or understanding? You shouldn't worry about Google AdSense. It is a clear-cut approach to monetize your blog while doing something you love.

Find A Blog Theme And Stick To It

Find yourself a Blogging Theme and stick to it. It is by far the best strategy when it comes to blogging, choosing your blog theme and how to use it properly can give you a great looking blog. By doing this, you can only get to know your theme well by using it again and again.

Choosing one theme over another is vital for your blog and stay with it. Some others have used some different themes for each of their blogs. Although this may be good to see which one fits your style or ideas best after a while, you'll have to work out what you have to know in detail about each theme to make it work the best for you. So each time you access each item, you'll have to remember a set of different features to maximize the theme's potential.

It will take time as well to learn all you can about how each theme works and how to maximize it's potential for your blog. After using some themes, it's best to use the one you feel most comfortable with. The one that's easy to use, upload images, videos and ads in a simple non-time consuming way.

It's easy to use and after a while and with a little practice anyone can use it to produce a great blog that offers a professional look and feel that some of the free themes don't. This theme provides some great ways to displays AdSense ads as well as banner ads. Posting images and videos is easy, and this theme offers a great affiliate program try it out and sees what you think.

CHAPTER 3

SUCCESS SECRETS YOU DIDN'T KNOW

What To Blog About?

Blogging has become a trendy thing, both in and out of the make money online niche. But most blogs run into a lot of trouble. If you want to be successful with blogging you need to know some of the problems people run into and how to not fall into those problems yourself.

The most significant type of trouble that blogs run into is, they don't get updated enough.

Or they don't get updated ever. What blogging burn out is a significant problem. It is a simple fact of life that not everyone is a writer. But almost everyone does have great ideas and thoughts to share. So why do blogs not get updated?

❖ Not knowing what to blog about

Something happens when people have thought and try to put it down on paper. Their brain goes blank.

Or if they are anything like me they always have great ideas and then forget them when they are in front of the computer.

❖ How do I pick a topic to blog about?

You can blog about anything, indeed anything. Blog about dogs, blog about cats, blog about how the clouds look out the window of your office building.

Here is a simple checklist to help you figure out if something is a good topic to blog about:

- ❖ Is this something I am interested in?
- ❖ Is this something I am knowledgeable about?
- ❖ If not is this something I am interested in enough to learn about?
- ❖ Would my friends be interested in this if we were talking about it in person?
- ❖ Do I think random people who would be interested in this?

If you answered yes to those questions, then blog it.

Find interesting topics to blog about

There are many ways to find topics that people find interesting so you can write a blog post.

❖ Social Media - Facebook, Twitter, Google+

If you are reading these chances are you have some form of social media. This is the best place to figure out what to blog about. Simply look at what your friends are posting. Are they talking about some celebrity? If so write about that celebrity. Then be sure to share your new blog post with your friends. Get them talking about your blog post in their social media. Not only will this give you exposure, but chances are also they are going to mention something that will spark a new idea.

❖ Yahoo Answers

Yahoo Answers is a place that people post questions and look for the internet to answer it for them. What better place to find out what people want to read about then looking at a site where people are asking questions? There are a ton of different categories to pick from. Just make sure you see in the types you are interested in. There is even a way to use Yahoo Answers to bring traffic to your blog that will be covered in a later blog post.

❖ Alexa What's Hot

Alexa is a company that tracks information about websites. Alexa tracks demographics of visitors, site traffic and more. One of the best things they do is monitor what gets searched for the most by users with their toolbar installed. If you know what people are searching for, you know what to blog about. You can even use the Alexa What's Hot to pull up the search results for those keywords.

Now that you have some places to get ideas, sit down, pick a topic and blog. As soon as you are done reading this, write your post. Action creates results.

Creating Good Website

A new upcoming standard in web marketing is blogging. Even smaller corporations and businesses are beginning to get blogs. A blog, short for WebLog, is a website that shows user created and published entries as posts in reverse chronological order, much like a web journal. It is fun and fasts to create a website for your blog, and it's also typically straightforward.

A blog is easy to maintain because once you have it set up, adding entries is a breeze after you write them. It also offers a way to interact with your customers, and potential customers, through comments. You can create a website for your blog with many different kinds of software and no need to labor over learning markup languages.

Before you start, you need a domain name. A domain name is a name that people use to reach your website, rather than a cryptic IP address. To create a website that is simple to find, you need to have a good domain name. You can choose from different registrars, companies selling domain names, to search their lists and see if the one you want is available. It takes a few tries to find a name which isn't taken yet, but it's worth it to get an easy to remember domain name related to your work.

You also need to have hosted so that there is a place to put your website files. Hosting is a service provided by a company that has a server connected to the Internet on which they will let you set the data for your website. Many registrars and Internet service providers also offer hosting services, and other companies offer only hosting. Hosting services can vary in price from free to over twenty dollars per month.

Now that you have a domain and a hosting service, you can get to the good part, creating a website for your blog. There are many types of blogging software to choose from, so you should download a few free trials and play around until you find the one that you like.

When you create a website, make sure to customize it by adding your company or personal logo and any other pieces of your brand such as custom colors. You want your blog site to be unique and memorable, so it impacts your visitors and encourages them to return. Once you have your blog set up the way you want it, make sure to update often to drive traffic to your website.

Avoid The Worst Way To Start

There is a method, if not done right, that stands out as the worst way to start. That way is the use of ads and banners.

Don't be a blogger that smothers your blog with ads. Ads are ugly and clutter a blog. Starting a blog with too many ads may turn off readers so much that they don't even bother to take a good look at what might be the real value of your blog and that is your valuable content. They may never attempt to come back to your blog.

The most annoying and irritating ads are pop up or pop down ads and flashing banner ads. It seems that banners, especially flashing banners, get less and less attention from readers these days. So if you want to make money blogging stay away from these irritating ads.

Having banners all over your blog is not a smart way to try to make money from blogging. Readers to your blog will know that these are just ads and won't even bother clicking on them. Instead, your readers may click out of your blog missing out on a chance to read your valuable content.

When was the last time you clicked on a flashing banner? Or if you did, it was only to delete the banner. Stay away from a pop-up or pop-down ads and flashing banner ads. They can hinder your blog more than help your blog. These can have an adverse effect as you try to make money with your blog. All that these nuisance ads may provide for you is zero commissions.

Starting a blog with those considerable AdSense block ads that are positioned between the blog post title and the post text of your blog is also not a good idea. They scream to the reader "these are ads" and can create a terrible first impression. You want your readers to read your blog posts immediately.

You don't want them leaving your blog before they get a chance to read your valuable content. If you are a blogger that wants to use AdSense ads, position them in smaller blocks or at the bottom of the post. A good tip is to go to Google's AdSense heat map to help with the positioning of these ads. With the AdSense heat map, you can get practical ideas as to how to select one or two ads to be placed strategically within your blog.

Smothering your blog with ads and just blasting them across your blog pages make your blog look unprofessional. The design of your blog suffers, and you may even lose credibility with readers. If you feel you must use ads and banners limit the amount you use. It will make your blog look much cleaner and reader-friendly.

Do You Have What It Takes?

Let's face it starting a blog is relatively straightforward. There are thousands of web hosts out there who are ready and willing to offer you blogging services. Also, you can use free hosting services such as Blogger or Wordpress. Many people start a blog with the intention of making income, but unfortunately, they approach the game with a completely wrong mindset.

There is an essential element that must be understood. A blog is not a business. A blog is simply put a self-promotional tool assisting you in making your business a success. Therefore thinking like a blogger is no good if you intend to build an income or build a business. To earn significant income from blogging you have to start thinking like an entrepreneur. It is not enough to be able to write compelling new content you have to look for ways of making this content pay.

The most important thing is to give your visitors real quality, write an article which they can apply in their life and really feel the benefit of them, not only will this increase your visitor loyalty it will also be a more fulfilling experience for you, as starting an online business should not just only be about making money.

Building Links, like any other website, to be noticed and receive traffic you have to get links to your site. It is an absolute must that you do this correctly.

It is what you now have to decide. Are you just going to be a good blogger? Are you going to create high content but have no real strategy for generating income from it? There is nothing wrong with this approach, but if you're looking to gain income, you have to be more strategic in your approach.

Updating your content and making sure it is of sound quality is essential but it is only part of the puzzle. You must have a plan for making sales or ultimately making money. A lot of bloggers do not know how to deal with the hidden complexities of making a substantial income from their blog. There are many aspects of dealing with if you want to give your business and income longevity.

Decide what products meet your target audience and how you can pitch them. Do you want to make a product of your own? Do you want to advertise on your site Whatever you plan to work your blog around it? Neither consumers nor advertisers will not want to invest in a product which is only half right. Content does not generate income, just as a new electronic device does not create sales. Marketing, pitching, reviewing and targeting are all needed to make any product sell.

When people find out you are trying to create an online business, there will be a certain amount of cynicism.

People will accuse of joining the dark side by trying to make a living from home. Peoples general perception is that it is a lazy way to make money when in reality it is anything but. Think of all the work you do to keep your content up to date, deal with the format of your site, promotion, article writing, researching, all this to give people the information they are searching for and to give it to them with such quality requires tremendous effort and patience.

There are also those who do not understand the potential for making money online, do not understand the concept of blogging for money and accuse you of dreaming or wasting your time. YES, you have to be patient, YES you have to work hard, but isn't having a job where you set your hours, wake up and your there, create a substantial amount of income worth it. If not stick to the 9-5.

What Causes Blogs To Fail?

The thing that most people find difficult with a blog is maintaining the supply of content over the long-term.

Fortunately, it is easy to prepare that content in advance of when you want it to appear on your blog, and this is a feature that will help you to get a lot more out of your marketing that you wouldn't be able to do with many other forms of marketing.

You could spend a day or two, or however long it takes, to create enough short blog posts to update your blog regularly throughout the year.

It is a lot easier than having to log in to your blog every few days or every week and come up with new content to add.

By doing it all at once you will have a good list of keywords and search terms, and you will have done all the research that is necessary to create good content in one sitting.

You can then prepare all your content and stay focused on developing that content, and then load it up to your blog with it scheduled to post into the future.

For most people, this is the only way to ensure that they will have a blog that stays active and continues to make money.

Obviously where there is less competition you won't need to update your content as often and in certain circumstances, you won't need to update your content at all if there is no competition, but these days with more and more people in the market it is generally necessary to have content appearing on a regular basis.

If you're targeting particularly small groups of keywords, then you can rework the same content to include those keywords in a manner that the content is not duplicate.

CHAPTER 4

FREE VS PAID OPTIONS TO MAKE MONEY BLOGGING

When you want to create a blog, you have one choice to make right off the bat. You need to decide if you are going to go with one of the many free platforms that are available out there or if you are going to pay to set yours up. There are many advantages and disadvantages to going with each of the different plans to start to make money blogging.

As you decide which route you are going to go with, there are many things that you want to keep in mind. Of course, the top thing on your mind is going to be what the balance in your bank account is and whether you can afford this. The good news is that even the paid format is relatively inexpensive so that should be easy to save up for and also to get your current financial situation to cover. Let's take a look at your two options to create a blog.

Free Blogs

Many different companies have platforms that can allow you to create a blog for free. The beautiful part about their being so many choices is that you can easily choose a layout from the available options that you like for your new venture. The look of your space on the Internet is essential when it comes to being able to make money from it.

You can get started posting your content and gaining traffic to it, without having to put any money in your plan. The only thing that you need to invest to make money is your time and hard work to create the revenue stream that you want.

The main disadvantage to using the free platforms is that the company that gave you the blog can also change its rule and take it down. There have been stories of free blogging platforms doing away with their blogs or just deleting blogs that they did not want on their site any longer.

Paid Blogs

To create a blog through a paid system, you will be paying for your domain name and hosting. These are not that great of an expense when you look into. Many people can set it all up for less than $20 a month to get everything that they need. Once you have paid, you own everything about your site. You do not have to worry about it getting deleted or someone changing the rules about what you can post. You can do as you please and grow your money making business as you like.

For some people, coming up with even the small amount of cash to create a blog in this way is too possible. They do not want to pay out money before they have even made a dime in revenue. For these people, the paid setup will not be for them no matter how much more creative freedom that you can have with it.

Learning What It Takes

To make money blogging sounds cool and the idea of working online from home makes this an even more attractive way to escape the rat race. It is important to recognize however that a money making blog is not something you directly plug into an outlet and wait for it to produce you an income! Many are not fully aware of what it takes to earn money blogging, but hopefully, our discussion here will help clear up any misunderstandings as to what they should expect.

For anybody interested in establishing money making a blog that will produce you a good income here are 5 'realities' as to what you should expect and plan for!

❖ Build It and They Will Come - NOT

Even though blogs are relatively simple to create and just as simple to maintain they do require your effort and on a consistent basis. The very first thing you will need to start growing your site is traffic. However, if you have little or no content why would anybody want to visit?

In the early stages, you will need to post frequently to your site to begin to attract attention, but you will also need to employ other traffic generation techni☐ues as well! The reason for this is your site has no 'history' meaning it is brand new therefore nobody knows it even exists, at least not yet! You need to get the word out!

❖ Posting is Essential

As mentioned above frequent posting is essential and most especially in the infancy stages of your site. As your blog 'mature' your posting schedule does not have to be as frequent, but you do want to be sure what you publish is of high quality. Remember if you want to earn money blogging you must be willing and able to 'deliver' useful and reliable information to your readers, and consistently.

Another note here is that you do want to continue using various traffic generation techniques. Even though your posts will attract new readers there are still some 'nooks and crannies' on the internet where people may not be alerted to your updates. It is up to you to bring your site to their attention!

❖ Blogs Are Living 'Entities'

Remember that blogging platforms are 'niche-specific' social sites that will involve plenty of interaction with visitors. Also, remember that there are other maintenance responsibilities you will need to tend to as well, therefore, plan on investing a lot of time in doing so. On a money making blog, maintaining contact with visitors is crucial since you are also expecting these people to make purchases on your site. The advantage a blog has over a website is that it is interactive therefore it only makes sense to use this advantage! Your contact lends reassurance to people considering making a purchase!

❖ Relationships Do Not Develop Overnight

When working online relationship building is essential, and this is especially true if you expect to earn money blogging. People who visit your site expect two things, to be supplied with worthwhile content and also to be able and interact with others.

Now if you take this to the next level where you expect these people to spend money on your site you want to be especially sure to make an effort to bond with them. It will help to increase the effectiveness of your marketing efforts dramatically. With that said these bonds will not be created overnight and will require your involvement to develop them.

❖ Earning Trust Comes Before Earning Income

As our conversation here has hopefully made clear so far, it will take time and effort first to develop traffic and then begin forging relationships. Your successful efforts will eventually lead to trust, and it is at this point that you will be able to earn money by blogging on a consistent basis. Remember however that the efforts we spoke of here today will need to be maintained consistently for you to rely upon your blog as a steady source of income!

It's Not Your Passion That Counts

One common teaching in the make-money-blogging ebooks is to follow your passion. If your objective in blogging is merely to express your knowledge or share your expertise with your readers, you may blog about your passion. But if your primary purpose for starting the blog is to monetize it, you have to follow the money.

To follow the money, you need to understand what people are searching for and are willing to pay for. Blogging is monetized through advertising and promotion: active or passive. You make money in blogging when you display ad links or banners; or when you promote other people's products.

If you display link ads or banners, you can be compensated by cost per click; per thousand of impressions; or per day, week or month that the ads are displayed on your site. For people to click on the ads, your readers should be interested in them because the ads match what they are looking for. You get paid because there are advertisers who are selling their products or services to your readers. Without the advertisers, you don't make money.

In promoting other people's products, on the other hand, you need to offer a solution to people's problems or pains; or answer their wants. So, first and foremost before starting your blog is to choose the niche that has reasonably good income potential.

Using the Google AdWords Keyword Tool which is free, you can see the number of average monthly searches that a particular product or service is getting globally. You can get a reasonably good idea of how many people are interested in it. There are other details that you need to look into if you're serious about making money blogging.

How much advertisers are willing to pay per click; and how competitive the keywords are, should be researched too. Starting with the right foundation, driving traffic into your site won't be as tricky as when only a few people are looking for your keywords.

So, as you can see here, it is not what you want that matters for you to make money blogging. What matters is what others need and want. Zig Ziglar said, "To get what you want, you have to help enough people to get what they want." To get a passive income through blogging, you need to answer enough number of people's needs or wants. If your objective is to make money blogging, you need to follow the money, not your passion.

Profit Potentially 5 Figure Monthly Income

The beauty of blogging is that anybody can start for literally less than 20$ and end up making 10,000$ a month in less than a year. It's not entirely comfortable, and most bloggers fail, but by reading the right advice and going along the correct path there's absolutely no reason why you shouldn't succeed.

❖ How to pull significant profit via Blogging

There are many things you have to do before you start pulling tons of money with blogging, but there are several things that you can do to ensure that you'll make the amount of money you need to.

Marketing - You ultimately want to make sure that you are marketing correctly, by learning how to sell your blog using methods such as social bookmarking, forum & message board posting, SEO, PPC, and even building up friendships and doing JV partnerships you can ultimately make a great deal of cash.

Monetizing - Affiliate programs, selling ad space, text links, Adsense, the possibilities are endless when it comes to monetizing your traffic. Just pick a niche or blog subject you love and start making money with it today, there's no reason why you can't succeed.

Building Up Long-Term Readers - Many people hate reading about building up lists and long-term readers because they do not have it yet!

So here's one thing you should do, you should think about getting one reader at a time, and trying to develop a good relationship with your readers in the beginning.

You can build a little community in the beginning with this blog. As time goes on you want to attract as many readers as possible, by having long-term readers; you'll be able to do things like recommending affiliate products on your blog posts or even your products people even have an online store that compliments their blog.

Do All The Plug-Ins Matter?

Having made hundreds of thousands of dollars using Blogger which doesn't have any plug-ins, and seeing dozens of people make similar incomes from WordPress by only using the default template and the default settings, it's evident that while plug-ins can help you, they are not necessary for you to succeed and make money by blogging.

The real reason people make money from blogging is not from the templates or the plug-ins that they use but more importantly from the market research and the keyword research that they do before they even start to create content.

And also, it is a promotion that they do for the blog that helps them to get traffic and thereby make money.

There is very little that you need to do to optimize a WordPress blog other than having your primary call to action in a prominent place so that your website visitors take the work that you want them to for you to make money.

Those are the most important things that you can do with your blog, not choosing a fancy template or seeing how many plug-ins you can put on your blog.

You need to focus on the basics of building a good business rather than trying to impress people with all the features of your blog.

It doesn't matter what you do or what you use. What matters is how much money you can make from what you are doing and how much time it takes you to earn that money.

Combining With Paid Advertising

You should always create your blogs in such a manner that you would be willing to spend money on advertising to send traffic to them.

If you don't believe you could make money from sending paid traffic to your blog, then you haven't correctly created your blog.

People who spend money on advertising know that they have to optimize the page that they are sending people to.

They need to know that the majority of the traffic they are sending will take the action that they want them to take to ensure that they make a good return on their investment.

Just because it doesn't cost you anything other than time to create your blog does not mean that it shouldn't be optimized in such a manner that it performs at its best.

Your time is valuable and your time is worth money so when you are creating a blog is assumed that you are paying for the people who come to that blog and make sure that you do all you can to get people to do what you want them to when they get there.

By just having this mindset you can increase your income considerably.

Another benefit of creating your blogs in such a manner is that the income that you can generate from them can then be invested and paid advertising to boost your business even more significant than it could be if you were merely relying on free search engine traffic.

If you create an excellent blog and you know that it is converting well, then you can start sending paid traffic knowing that it will also translate well.

It's the best of both worlds.

CHAPTER 5

DEBUNKING MYTHS ABOUT MAKING MONEY BLOGGING

Blogging can get very mind boggling at times, and there are so many factors like comments, likes, tweets, traffic, content, social media and numerous other little things that can increase one's anxiety to a dangerous level.

If you Google tips & tricks for blogging, you will receive numerous results telling what to do and what not do, and with so many suggestions by endless professional and amateur bloggers, the difference in opinion is inevitable; which leads to even greater confusion. So here are 5 basic myths that will help in clearing some doubts that you may have been debating about:

Myth 01: You can write about anything

Sure you can write about anything, but this theory holds true when you are starting your blog and deciding what to write about. But once you've started you need to be a little more focused and concentrate on the theme of your blog. Freedom of speech is a luxury in blogging, but if you wish to receive consistent traffic, then you need to stick to a niche. Going off the track is acceptable once in a while, but you can't be writing about elections one day and gardening the other.

Myth 02: Good Content = Popular Blog

There is a thin line between being good and being famous. It is true that content is the king, but that does not necessarily mean that your blog will become popular automatically. Apart from writing good content and giving useful information, you need to make sure that you make people aware of it and this is where marketing or promoting your blog comes into the picture.

Don't just sit there and expect people to find you on their own because there are much fish in the sea. But the good news is that once people do see you and realize how good your content is, they will keep coming back.

Myth 03: Blogs Are About Writing Only

There are so many things that you can blog about, and you will find that there are many blogs that speak through picture or videos. It doesn't matter how you share, and it's about what you share.

You will find that many bloggers share what others have written (of course by giving due credit to the author), while there are some who share links rather than publishing an entire post. By the end of the day, your blog is your baby, and you don't have to stick to a particular format every time, and that's the beauty of blogging.

Myth 04: You Have To Post Daily

It is a prevalent practice that many bloggers consider as a fundamental of blogging, but then again it's the quality that counts and not the quantity. But this doesn't mean that you end up delaying posting and give lengthy gaps between posts, you need to be constant.

You can write 3-4 times a week or even once a week, but stick to a schedule so that your readers know when to visit your blog to find something new. If you are not posting daily, then make it a point that you spend some time responding to comments on your blog and promoting your blog through various channels.

Myth 05: Negative Comments Will Ruin My/Company's Reputation

The fact is that your readers will not always be careful; they may criticize or disagree with you and express it in very harsh ways at times. They may not like what you have written or how you've written something, but it's not their comments that will determine your reputation instead it's how you respond to these comments. Don't take it personally and provide authentic information, if you think that someone has a point in what they are saying then acknowledge it graciously. Think of it as an opportunity to interact with your readers and engage them in meaningful conversations.

Fundamental Elements Of Success

Blog marketing is becoming an increasingly important element to your overall blogging success. Today, it is not only good enough that you write high-quality content, but it is just as critical that you have an action plan to get your voice heard among the other 100 million plus blogs!

If you are thinking about starting a blog or if you already have a blog, there are a few things you need to do to become a dominant player in your category.

❖ Write original, high-quality content.

It seems obvious, but often time people start a blog with the best of intentions and soon realize that it takes some work. Soon they get lazy and begin to fill their blog with RSS feeds from others.

❖ Update on a regular basis.

Everyone's approach is a bit different, but the key is to update on a "consistent" basis. Bloggers are advised to tell readers up front what your usual schedule is for new posts. The key is to set the expectation in the reader's mind and then be consistent. It will show professionalism on your part and also help to prove yourself as an authority.

❖ Have a well-defined niche.

It is an important point, and it is becoming more critical every day. By "niche," this is about a distinct specialty within your market. For example, if you have a topic about dogs, it is too broad of a topic and challenging to get noticed in the search engines.

However, let's say your topic is about breeding poodles. The theme is much more specific and allows you to target your marketing efforts precisely. You have a total smaller market, but much more meaningful and responsive to your material.

Focusing On Your Forte

When people decide to try and make money blogging, they think that they can spend an hour or two in front of their computer and wait for the check to come in the mail.

The whole process of earning with blogging is not as easy as snapping your fingers. While established pro bloggers can achieve this feat later in their lives, newcomers have to shed some serious blood, sweat, and tears to grasp the fundamentals of blogging.

You do not merely bash your keyboard and expect people to read whatever comes out. You need to give your blog some serious thought before you even sit down and begin typing.

And this is where your Forte comes in.

❖ Defining your forte

Everyone knows a thing or two about something, but only an expert knows everything about something. You have to know everything about something. Find a topic that you like, that you know, and that you can share with others. A specific music genre, the hottest online game, the current financial crisis, the real estate market in California and even something as disgusting as the ins and outs of fecal matter is all fair game for you to blog about, so get cracking and find a forte for you to focus on.

❖ Strengthening your forte

You may know everything about something, but that can change with each passing second. You earn with blogging by sharing something with your readers that they do not already know, and you need to keep your knowledge up-to-date and razor sharp if you want to hold on to your audience. The mark of a true professional is increasing your competencies. It also applies to blog, so you must spend a significant amount of time and effort honing your forte.

❖ Diversifying your forte

Knowing everything about something only works for blogs if that something appeals to people. Freshness and originality are the secret ingredients for you to profitable blogging.

While you can restrict your knowledge into one particular niche, you can expand your knowledge by trying your hand in a new experience. By diversifying your forte, you can explore other potential areas for your understanding to be applied in. It not only strengthens your forte but allows you to think outside the box and come up with new content for your blog.

❖ Writing your forte

You may know everything about something, you may be up to date with it, and you are coming up with fresh new content all the time. That will be worth squat if you do not know how to write. The basic requirement for blogging is writing skill, and that supersedes your knowledge.

You need to present your information in a reader-friendly format, and this is why you need to invest a little time and effort in honing your language and writing skills.

Grammar and spelling errors kill the credibility of your discussion, so remember to keep them in check if you do not want your readers' eyes to bleed out of their sockets. Define your forte, strengthen it, diversify it and then write it down. These are the basic requirements to make full use of your knowledge to make money blogging, so keep them in mind when you go off to make your fortune in the beautiful world of writing.

Free Traffic And Backlink To Blog

Before you begin to start this idea of blogging to make money, you must have a lot of patience. You can use Blogger.com to make your blog. It is straightforward to use, and the basic layouts are great for your viewers to see. If you are planning to make money, do not use the standard free URL that Blogger gives you, for example, yourblog.blogspot.com. It does not look professional, and search engines (Google, Yahoo, etc.) do not like that. You can spend $10 to buy a domain name, and that will last you a year, but you can always renew it.

Now you have a blog, and you need to submit your blog to a bunch of search engines. The three big search engines are Google, Yahoo, MSN. You can send to other search engines as you wish. It is an essential step because most of your blog's traffic will come from search engines. Again, in my very first sentence, you need a lot of patience because getting your blog indexed to search engines might take weeks or months. Sign up for networking websites. A few popular ones are Delicious, Twitter, and StumbleUpon. You can search for people with similar blogs as you. If you are blogging about making money, search for people who are also blogging about how to make money. Add them to your network, and some of them will add you back to their network. Don't expect everyone you add to your network to add you back into their network. Also, visit these people's blogs and make some intelligent comments. Do not just say, "great blog!"

Post in your blog frequently. If you want to make money, you have to get in the habit of posting a lot on your blog. Make sure you ping your blog every time you have a new post.

A good ping site is pingomatic.com. They will help you announce to other people that your blog has been updated. Sign up for feedburner.com too because they are a great source to spread the words out about your blog. However, feedburner.com does not like inactive blogs so make sure you post frequently.

Try to write an original article at least once a week that is not in your blog, and then submit that article to a high page ranking publishing website. Do not copy and paste an article from your blog because search engines do not like duplicates. The purpose of publishing articles to these websites is to get readers to visit your website and get good quality backlinks.

Make sure you have an e-mail address up top somewhere in your blog because once you get a lot of traffic to your site, there will be people trying to contact you about advertising on your site.

It is essential! If people cannot contact you, you will be missing out opportunities to make money. After all, your blog is about making money. Sign up for Google AdSense for additional income. Set it up to be somewhere up top in your blog, but don't make a giant billboard Google ads because viewers find those annoying. Just a little box would be beautiful.

More Traffic, More Leads, More Money

Do you want to know the very first thing you should do whenever you start a new online business?

It's so easy that you will wonder why you didn't think about it. Start any new business with a blog. It's that simple.

❖ Why should you do that?

Because your business will be up and running within minutes. It's much easier to start a blog than creating a website from scratch.

❖ What blog platform should you use?

If you are on a budget, it is recommended to start with a free blog like blogger.com. If you can invest in a web hosting, you should start right away with a wordpress.org blog that you will set up on your server. Another reason why you need to have your blog is that Google, Yahoo and Msn love blogs. You can make a post, ping it to a service like pingoat.com, and drive traffic to your new posts in minutes.

Another compelling reason why you should have a blog is that you can easily interact with people in your niche. When your visitors and subscribers read your blog, something magic happens. They feel that they know you, and you can gain their trust. It is essential that your potential customers trust you because if they don't, they will not buy from you.

3 Principles Of Every Successful Blog

Starting a blog is not a set and forget kind of thing. You need to invest your time gradually to get growing results. If you are confused about what to do to move on the right track, here are a few tips that can help you.

1. Place strategy above all

Don't try to align your strategy around a specific feature of a blog. If the blog doesn't allow you to post audio or video, but these multimedia contents are part of your strategy, you should switch to other blog platforms or find ways to extend the functionality. A blog is a tool to help you accomplish something, in this case communicating with your readers, prospects, and customers. You should think about art you want to hang on the wall first and then find the tool (hammer and nail) to do the job.

It may sound like common sense, but I'd tell you it's not common practice at all. If you find yourself shopping for a blog theme first without knowing what you're going to do with your blog clearly, you are making this very mistake.

2. Plan a content strategy

Content is the lifeblood of every blog. You should have a strategy about it. What types of readers you want to attract, how to get them to your blog, how you cultivate the relationship, etc.

You also need to consider the personality that you convey through the content. Without a strategic plan, you are going nowhere, no matter how bright your destination is.

Here's what you can do. Write 5-10 pillar articles, excellent content, that are going to be the center of your blog. New visitors who come to your blog will find these and read them. They will make decisions whether to subscribe to get more stuff from you based on the quality of these articles.

3. Align the design

There are one, two, there and even four column layouts for your blog. Some of them include a big header, and others allow you to have lots of ads. You can also emphasize on the guest blogger's name. Your design should align with your strategy.

Bloggers should change their layout to optimize the user experience instead of to make the site looks modern and new. Remember, a strategy first. Although the design is essential, if it drives the readers away from your goal, you should go against it.

With so many unique designs out there, you can almost get what you want. In case you can't, some web designers are affordable too.

CHAPTER 6

THINKING OF MAKING MONEY?

Blogs Are Key

You'd have to be blind and deaf not to have noticed people making money blogs. These are blogs that are kept for the sole purpose of generating income. If you're thinking of jumping onto the bandwagon and making money from your blog, there are two ways to do it.

Do it yourself. Under this scheme, it's all you. You look for a niche to tailor your blog around, and you do keyword research (what's the point of having a blog if it's not optimized?), then you think up blog topics and write a short article, about 300-500 words, on these topics daily.

The whole point of a blog is that it is updated regularly, so it's crucial to create content every day. Then there's article directory submission. You want both humans and spiders to pay attention to your blog, so naturally, you should create some link juice for your site.

Let others do it for you. Beyond writing daily blog entries to keep your site updated, you will need to position your blog so that people looking for information on topics you are writing about will find you. And when they do, you want to keep their interest so that they will remember your blog and visit it regularly.

Ultimately, you want them to subscribe to your content. How cool is it to have people receive email updates every time you update your blog? Very! But that can only happen if you have something worth following. Interesting, useful content should be matched with visibility. That's how you build a following. When you can do that successfully, you'll have a blog that can make you money. Then, and only then, can you say that your money blogs work?

Find A Hot Niche To Make Easy Money

Make money blogging is considered as an alternative to the conventional online business model. This particular business model became popular after Matt Mullenweg share WordPress, the free blogging script. The big question is how to make money blogging. Internet Gurus have tried to figure out the answer to this question. They, who have already gain success, share the blueprint of their success stories.

To make money blogging you should understand that it is not black magic or sort of things; it requires time and effort to achieve that target. The most critical point of this entire idea is the keyword research.

You should master the keyword research before going any further into the other process such as building blogs, writing a blog post, monetizing the blog, and marketing your blog. Mastering this concept, you can easily spot a right keyword which has at least 10,000 searches per month and has less than

200,000 competitions. This kind of keyword usually called niche keyword. The niche keyword will enable you to target a specific niche market.

To begin with, here are two proven ways you can use to find a hot niche.

First, you should use the Google search box and the AdWords keyword tool. Insert the keyword you want to use; do not forget to use the quotes. The Google search box will provide the result of keyword competition level. On the other hand, the AdWords keyword tools will provide the searches volume. From those statistics, you should be able to locate a hot niche which has the criteria as mentioned above.

The second way is by finding niches backward. This method is a combination of blog and affiliate marketing. The main idea of this method is to find the affiliate product first and build a blog to promote this particular product.

After choosing the product, you have to apply the same keyword research strategy to maximize your keyword performance. As described above, the keyword research strategy will lead you to find the appropriate niche keyword related to your affiliate product.

Outsourcing

Once you've started to generate a reasonable amount of money from your blogging, and provided you have kept everything simple, you will be able to start outsourcing a lot of the work.

Outsourcing is the cheap way to get the mundane tasks done so you can concentrate on the other aspects of your business that need more expertise such as the market and keyword research. Once you free up your time from doing these menial tasks, you'll find that your business will go ahead in leaps and bounds.

You can get quality content created for very little expense, and that content can be built around keyword lists that you supply to your workers. It would give you the ability to create mini nets of blogs where you might not have had the time if you were doing all the work on your own.

It does pay to create a system that is simple that not only you can manage efficiently but you can easy train your outsource workers to manage thereby freeing up more of your time.

Unless and until you have a simple system that can be followed you will not be optimizing your work, and you will not be able to optimize the work that you give to outsource workers.

Initially, it might only be the content creation that you get them to do that as they get more familiar with your business you'll be able to get them to create your blogs and the other aspects of the company provided they understand it correctly.

If you create a simple template that works, you will be able to give them this template, and they will be able to upload that when they create the blog.

All of these little things will save you a lot more time and in doing so make you more money for less effort.

Fact Or Fiction?

It depends on you. Can you make money online by blogging? The answer is a resounding yes! The key to making money blogging has a lot to do with the following factors. They are all critical to your success.

1. Unique Content: Lots Of It- You are not going to get very much standing in the search engines if you do not put up original content. If you do not want to write fresh content, you need to have a budget to have someone else do this for you. If you do not have anything unique and exciting to share with your audience, they will leave you very quickly. You need to be a content generation machine to get a blog running correctly. It is an essential part of your success, and there's no way to avoid this. It is best to start to plan on how you are going to get your content done.

2. Solutions To Problems- You do not want just to put up random "stuff" on your blog. You want to have a content plan. You want to engage your audience and provide solutions to their problems. If you are going to provide solutions to problems, you need to know what you are talking about and have some real-world experience to back you up.

It is why your choice of a niche for your blog is such a critical decision. If you want to teach people how to do something, it is best that you can do it yourself. *"Fake it till you make it"* approaches are just not a good idea, as your readers will figure out pretty quickly that you do not know what you are talking about. You are an expert in some area. It is the area you can blog about.

3. Persistence- Most people quit before they even get their blog started properly. Like any venture, you need to have at least a 90-day plan. You need to build and nurture your blog and start to develop a relationship with your readers. It is not going to happen in two weeks. If you are persistent, you will make steady progress. Do not try to take shortcuts in your blog development. Just do the work, and you will get your just rewards down the road.

4. Consistency- You should strive to put content on your blog in a steady, predictable manner. It is best for your visitors and the search engines. You will get a lot more positive results by posting over time as compared to a large "dump" of information at one time. Keep in mind you want to engage your audience and keep them coming back for more details. The best way to do this is to add content to your blog on a weekly basis pretty much as long as you want to keep the blog active and profitable.

5. Patience- This is the hardest one of all. If you commit to building a quality blog that is well organized with quality content, you will see some success. The key is to be patient enough to allow results to happen.

The only way you will not see some success is to quit posting on your blog. It is unfortunate that most people do quit trying on their blogs before they even have a reasonable chance to see success. Stay the course for 90 to 180 day, and you will have a tangible asset that can make you income for years to come.

Some Great Suggestions

Learning how to make money with a blog is very exciting and easy to do (if you know how). People all over the world are making a great living online by blogging and so can you! If you love to write and don't mind doing a little bit of research from time to time, then you are well on your way to blogging success.

So, how exactly can you make money from blogging?

Well, there are many different ways to monetize your blog...

1) You can sell advertising space on your blog;

2) You can sell products and services on your blog;

3) You can use AdSense or other advertising ad platforms on your blog;

4) Build a following of subscribers and sell services and products to them;

5) You can sell your blog (some people will pay you a nice little price if your blog is popular and well visited);

6) You can even sell your list of subscribers.

These are all fantastic ways to monetize your blog but what else can you do to make money with a blog?

Well, with this approach it's not necessarily your blog that you have to worry about making money with. Another great way to make money blogging online is by writing blog entries/posts for OTHER Blog sites!

That's right, and there are many blog owners out there who have big authority sites and do not have the time to keep them updated, so they pay other keen bloggers to keep their sites filled with fresh quality content. They pay you per post, and some sites even pay you for reviews of product and services!

So as you can see, there are many great ways on how to make money with a blog! All you have to do is to implement them.

CHAPTER 7

THE FASTEST WAY TO POSITIVE CASH FLOW

Begin With A Free Blog Site

You want to begin on your journey to bringing in some extra cash online, and you've decided to try blogging. If you've performed a little research, then you might have begun to wonder if you should use a free blog site, like Blogger or Wordpress, or if you should get your domain and host the blog on a website. So what's the answer?

Let's examine the advantages of both free blog sites and having your blog hosted on your own paid site.

Advantages of a free blog site

❖ Not only can you have one free blog, but you can also have unlimited free blogs
❖ More comfortable to get listed in search engines - especially with Google when using Blogger
❖ Ease of adding revenue tools like AdSense
❖ Don't have to worry about website design or HTML
❖ Advantages of hosting a blog yourself
❖ More freedom with customizing the design
❖ Some feel that it adds a more professional appearance

You can see from the above that there are more advantages to using free blogs. It is especially true when you're just starting out and have a limited budget with which to begin. The fact that the blogs are free through sites like Blogger makes it even easier for you to make money blogging since you don't have any overheard except for the time involved to write.

❖ Make Money Blogging

Your goal is to earn money through blogging. If you have no expense and you're making money with your blog, then you're indeed expanding your profit margin more than if you're paying for the site.

Business Tips To Help You Succeed

If you want to make money blogging, there is good news. While it is easy to start a blog, it will take some good advice to get you on the right track once you do start one. Here is what you need to know.

Having a blog does not mean that you will instantly be seen by thousands of readers. If you don't go about it the right way, there is a good chance that you will just be wasting your time, writing for only your eyes. You need to be familiar with keywords, well-written blog posts, and how to get the word out about your blog. All of this is a must if you want to make money blogging.

We will first talk about writing valuable content for your readers. We will assume that you have found a niche that you are pretty passionate about. If you have not found your blog's niche, please, take an hour so and write down all of the things that you are passionate about and go from there. You need to know what your readers want to know.

You need to think while stepping inside of their shoes. They have questions, and it is your job to provide the answers, or at the very least, tell them where they can find the answers.

While it is always a good idea to give your readers exactly what they want, it is also a great idea to write with entertainment value. Don't be afraid to be conversational. Most of your readers will want to read a laid-back, informative blog post. It will attract readers to your blog and have them coming back for more.

Who knows, they might even tell their friends about it. It should give you a good idea of how to approach writing for your readers. If you need extra help, the best way to study this subject is to see how some of the top bloggers so it. Scan Wordpress and look at how to Big Guns write their blogs. You will get a chance to see exactly what works.

Now we will talk about driving traffic to your blog. There are many ways to do this, but the most effective and fastest ways are the following:

Use The Right Keywords - You should have your whole blog revolve around a great keyword phrase. You don't want to pick keywords that are too popular, because you are just starting out, and you might get lost on the back pages of the search engine results. You want to pick keywords that have a good bit of searches but don't have much competition. You can use the Overture keyword tool to find the right keywords, and you can also browse the Google keyword tool. You can find these websites by typing in "Overture keyword tool" into a Google search box.

Post Comments - Another great way to drive traffic to your blog is to post comments on other peoples blog. It will give you valuable backlinks, and it will also entice readers to head on over to your blog. Make sure you are posting comments on blogs that have something to do with your blog's niche.

Article Writing - Another way to drive traffic to your blog is to write articles about your blog's subject. You are reading an article right now and you most likely found it through a search engine, right? If you did find this article through a search engine, you now see how powerful an article can be.

You want to make money blogging, but you might have thought that is an impossible task. After reading this, it should make you feel much better about writing a blog for profit. It involves a few simple tasks and the rest you will learn as you get involved in the blogging community and learn from the professionals. If you had doubts about how to make money blogging, you shouldn't now.

Your Mini Blueprint

You can make money blogging if you have a simple blueprint that shows you correctly what to do from beginning to end. It is a mini blueprint you can use for starters.

1. First, make sure your niche has a variety of products and services being marketed by your competition. Browse some of your competitor's websites using Google, Yahoo, and Bing, and see what they are selling. If you find people selling ebooks, videos, audios, courses, membership sites, you know you have a niche with a buying market. It is the most crucial piece of the blueprint. You MUST have a niche where people are buying various types of products and services.

2. Once you know there is an opportunity to make money in your niche, create an introductory product to build credibility with your customers. Your first product can be a 100-page eBook that you sell for $47 or you can create a series of videos/audios and sell them for $47. Just make sure you pick a product that you will have an easy time creating.

3. Create a second product a few months later and put a higher price tag on it. This product can be an advanced version of your first product or some type

of course that you sell for $97 or more. This product should be promoted to the people who purchased your first product. Approximately 10-to-20 percent of these people will buy your second product because you have built trust and credibility with them.

4. Next, create some training course with a higher price tag than your second product. Your training course can run for 60 days, and each week you teach a different subject online using web conferencing services. Again, you want to promote your training course heavily to the people who bought your first and second product for higher conversion rates.

Repeat this process until you have at least three different products or services in your sales funnel. As you continue to create products that solve peoples problems, you will notice that a small handful of people who read your blog buy everything that you sell. As a result, you will make money that far exceeds what most people are making online.

Proven Website Traffic Tips

There are several ways to properly build a successful blog that can attract tons of targeted buying traffic. You can offer a product, service or an entertainment theme. It doesn't matter. What is very important is that you utilize that traffic in ways that will help you to make money from blogging.

And with the vast array and of Internet offers for your blog including powerful, yet easy to use plug-ins, this will save you incredible amounts of time and money. It will make it easier for you when starting a home business. Always remember to be careful when choosing and optimizing your blog so that it can grow for many years to come.

Paying for advertising would be the easiest route to go, but the problem is that most new website owners do not have the monetary resources large companies do. But don't let that get you down. There are quick ways to make money even if you are on a budget.

First and foremost, you must do some research and start reading great blogging and SEO articles if you want to get organic traffic that is free. It doesn't have to be boring. The first three pages of Google, Yahoo, and Bing can give you great articles to learn from that are proven to work.

One way is typing your keyword such as "work from home business opportunities" or your blog niche into Google, Yahoo or Bing along with the word "articles." You will have thousands and thousands of written articles at your fingertips to help educate you to make money by blogging.

So, here are 3 ways of acquiring targeted website traffic while making money with blogs:

1. Writing Articles That Captures The Attention Of Your Reader

Try to pick an interesting topic in your niche that thousands of person would possibly enjoy reading such as making money blogs. Make sure to offer excellent tips on how they can benefit from your information, product or service.

Again, one of the easiest ways to start writing new articles is to read what others have written in the past on your subject and then re-write it with a twist or update it with proven strategies. It works. On the other hand, never, ever copy another author's article. It is pure laziness and is considered plagiarism.

After your article is written, include one or two links in the resource box back to your money websites or better yet a landing page to capture their name and e-mail.

The resource box is your short advertisement of your company telling people why they should read more on your product or service and in time, this will help you to make money by blogging.

2. How An Autoresponder Goes Hand In Hand With Your Newsletter

Let's try something new. Start sending some of your traffic to your link that is a landing page or a capture page. You can then request the reader's name and e-mail address by using an autoresponder in return for more information or a complimentary e-book or gift.

Now you are in a position to communicate with this new found reader who may become your new customer. You can then send them more offers in the future. Once they trust you and enjoy your newsletter, they will in time become your customer.

Remember to make your newsletter informative and fun. Unless you are discussing heart surgery, keep it down to earth and engaging. If you accomplish this, you will see your newsletter database of clients start increasing and your sales going up now and in the future. It will make starting a home business fun.

3. Using Affiliate Programs To The Full To Make Quick Money

Now that you have traffic coming to your blog or website, you can now make money fast online by offering other people's products or services through your affiliate link.

After you capture your reader's name and e-mail address, then you can send them to an affiliate page where you get credit each time a reader buys a product or service. By joining these affiliate programs, they will keep records of your transactions, bill your new client and handle all this automatically for you.

These companies will pay you a percentage of each sale while you do the marketing. Besides, you will save a lot of time by not having to create your product. Merely sell other people's products and take the money to the bank. It is a fun way to make money online blogging.

Powerful Concepts You Should Grab

During the last few years, so many new and different opportunities have shown up into our new millennium. And too many people haven't realized these yet. It will show you how to make money with a blog in a smart and fast way.

When you are exhausted, and you have had enough of the old concept of working "Exchange Time For Money," you should look at the Internet how the Holy Grail. It is the smart and fast solution to earn money blogging.

But you have to know 2 important things:

1 - The Right Knowledge;

2 - The Right Action;

Let us explain these 2 powerful concepts.

"The Right Knowledge" it means the most incredible and true information about how to make money with a blog and how to earn money blogging. Instead "The Right Action" it means to put together a proved successful strategy that guides you toward your financial freedom and pursuing it.

How to grab these 2 powerful concepts and to start a blog with success, intelligence, and great vision, is pretty significant because is the difference between who makes money online and who not.

In fact when is a time of starting a blog and try to figure out how to make money blogging, very often happens too many people don't know where and how to begin. There are too many information out there and understand which are better and which are the best, can be pretty tricky. So, it is essential don't be overwhelmed by information and should be careful during the process to design your blog and make sure to make your blog irresistible and exciting at the eyes of your readers.

CHAPTER 8

90 DAY PLAN

You want to make money blogging and are looking to get started. When can you expect to see some results? It is a common question. A good rule of thumb is if you work hard and work smart you can start to see some good results in about three months.

However, this is just your first milestone. It is when you start to see money coming in, but it is the beginning of something much bigger. When you get to his point, you are on your way to building something substantial that will pay you well into the future. If that appeals to you, then please consider the following tips:

1. **Thirty-day goal** -- This is where you lay the foundation. At the end of this phase you will have your site up and your beginning content complete. You will also have a procedure for linking as well as having some quality products and services to endorse.

2. **Sixty-day goal** -- This is where you kick it into a higher gear. You have laid the foundation and are ready to get things rolling. It is the time to pump out the content and shift your linking into high gear. The linking work you do during this time will result in lots of traffic. The content you are cranking out will be necessary for all of the new visitors that will be coming to your site.

3. **Ninety-day goal** -- By now you have the hang of it. The traffic is good, and you have started a solid base of loyal visitors. Soon you will begin to develop a relationship with your readers.

It is where the magic starts to happen. Now is the time that your readers begin to purchase the products you are recommending. Money is flowing in, and you are in a position to fine tune and improve. At this point, you are on your way to making money blogging for years to come.

Don't expect things to happen overnight. Know to go in that it will take about three months to get where you want to be. Be patient and stay focused. Set your goals and be consistent. If you can do this for three months, you will be in a position to have a valuable blog that will pay you handsomely for years to come.

The Secret Only A Few Know

Are you looking for blogging tips to make money blogging?

You don't have to search for long before you find a lot of products claiming how easy it is to make money if you only use this or that specific system.

Which product should you choose? What system will work?

Many of them will probably work if you employ the system the right way, and this is where the big secret comes into the picture.

The BIG secret is that you need to understand that blogging is not about you, it's about helping others.

Next time, you visit a blog, ask yourself: What am I doing here? Why am I reading this particular blog?

Your answer will probably be that you learn something from the blog. Or you get a giggle out of their jokes and funny pictures.

At any rate - you get something from the blog. If you don't, you'll leave and never return.

But there's more to it. Look at how your favorite bloggers address you. They are speaking directly to you, and they use the word "you" instead of "persons" or "readers."

When you're writing blog posts, make sure you talk to one person, your ideal reader. Blogging is a one-to-one conversation.

And there are so many choices out there. Just like TV shows... You can browse from station to station until you find something interesting. And in the second the show gets boring, you can leave it and find another one.

TV channels specialize, and you should do the same. Travel channels, for instance, target people who are keen on travel topics. They are not targeting sports enthusiasts at the same time.

Don't aim at targeting everybody. If you speak in general, your reader will not get the impression that you're addressing him. He will look around and see a crowd, and feel like being just a small member of it.

You need your readers to feel special.

Don't write for people interested in pets, but to women, aged 50, who owns a Siamese cat. That woman will feel that you talk directly to her if you address her that way.

The Reality Of Earning Through Online Blogging

Blogging is a hobby and one of the most popular methods of making money online. The setup sounds very simple: you write about something exciting and people will start visiting your website every day. You post some advertisements or sell some products in your blog and revenue starts rolling in as people start buying products or as ads are exposed to a lot of people. While the thought where you can make money blogging because of advertisements and product selling sounds like a good idea, the reality is different. You can set up a website; write something interesting about a topic, but the chances of getting people to visit your site are very minimal without additional effort.

Factors that Improves Website Visibility

Getting the attention of readers online may not be your ultimate goal, but it's a significant factor to increase your website's ability in money making. Online, every visitor is significant as they will help in improving your visibility as they continue to read what you write and possibly recommend your content to their friends.

The most critical factor in increasing visibility is the content. The adage, "content is king" is popular among online writers. Your online visitors will stop going back to your site if you don't have something new and exciting to say. Search engines such as Google, Yahoo, AOL, and Bing also value content.

Another essential factor to improve your site status so that you can make money blogging is linking to other sites. This factor is very tricky because you can't just place the link of your site anywhere. You need to have some valuable comments on various blogs and ask other webmasters to promote your site as you encourage theirs. This practice is called "link exchange" and one of the popular methods to increase awareness which can propel your website's capability for money making. An online presence can drastically improve as your web address is displayed on other sites.

❖ Expertise, Preferences, and Niche

Expertise, preferences, and niche are the ultimate tools on how to make money blogging. A niche will allow you to make money online as you become an expert on something unique and rarely found online. Also, if you're considering creating a website with a huge potential for earning, online preferences of readers should also be considered. When you expertly write about something they like which is unique to your site, you have a big chance of earning through your blogs.

Importance Of Blogging And 10 Ways Of Increasing Targeted Traffic

Have you ever asked yourself how a single person keeps on updating his blog with fresh content regularly without running out of ideas? Some bloggers will leave you to wonder how they manage to write content regularly. No one can dispute their prolific writing skills. Becoming a blogger is all about learning how to blog. Blogging isn't difficult as some people may tend to think. Below are four most important blogs that will teach you how to blog and how you can become a better blogger.

1.) Blogtyrant.com

2.) Copyblogger.com

3.) Problogger.net/blog

4.) Bloggingtips.com

If you're starting a freelancing writing business, then Freelancefolder.com blog will significantly help you with advice on how to go about your freelancing writing business.

Any person who is computer literate can now create a blog. You don't have to worry about the technical aspects since there are blogging software such as WordPress and Empower Network that have simplified blogging.

Importance of Blogging

1.) Blogging is Interesting: There is something that you love doing (your passion). Go ahead and create a blog and start blogging about your passion. Blogging will make you learn more about your passion. You'll be surprised by the attention you'll be receiving from people.

2.) Proper Usage of Free Time: Blogging isn't a waste of time. If it was a waste of time, we could not be having so many blogs currently. Instead of you being idle during most of your free time, you should create a blog and start blogging. It will make you not to question yourself on what you should do to keep yourself busy whenever you have free time.

3.) Inspiring Others: Blogging has made it possible for people to encourage one another even though they have never met each other. People share problems and support one another. For instance, here is a quote that shows how blogging has made it possible for a person to get support from people, *"I was having problems with depression and anxiety disorder, and it felt like not blogging about it was creating a false history. When I did finally share the problems I was having, I was shocked -not only by the support that was given to me but also by the incredible amount of people who admitted they struggled with the same thing."*- **Jenny Lawson**

4.) Making Money Online: Start blogging to earn some money online if you haven't found your dream job. There are many opportunities online that you can use your blog to make money. You can start blogging for money by being hired as a blogger. You can use your blog to do affiliate marketing, or you can use your blog to sell products to people online.

The opportunities to make money online from a blog are just many. It is upon you to decide on how you're going to make money online blogging.

5.) Gaining Exposure and Attracting Prospective Employers: Blogging exposes you as an expert in your field. You'll be recognized as an expert when you share informative information on your blog and also on other blogs that allow guest blogging. Some people will seek your advice while there are those who will refer people to read your articles.

Blogging will also expose your talent, creativity, passion and your dedication. *"Blogging is a great way to show your talents and interests to prospective employers while adding an edge to your resume. If you blog consistently it shows your dedication, passions, and creativity-all of which are key attributes employers look for in job candidates."-* **Lauren Conrad**

6.) Blogging Improves Your Writing Skills: When you keep on blogging, with time you become a better writer. You'll learn how to express yourself better. Blogging improves your writing skills and also your skills to communicate with people.

7.) Marketing and Building Relationships with Customers: Blogging is essential in marketing. A blog is a marketing tool, and marketers should use blogs to inform people about the products they're selling.

Marketers should blog informative information about the products they're marketing so that people know how such products are going to be useful to them in solving various problems. Blogging builds better relationships between customers and businesses.

Ten Ways of Increasing Traffic

Driving targeted traffic to your blog is a process that should be continuous. Here are ten ways that you can use to drive targeted traffic to your blog.

1.) Update Your Blog Regularly: You should start updating your blog regularly with fresh content that is unique and informative if you haven't been doing that.

2.) Quality Content and Not Quantity Content: Although you should update your blog with fresh content, it doesn't mean that you should update it with any content for the sake of updating it regularly. High-quality content is essential in retaining your existing targeted traffic. Posting high-quality content will make people visit your blog since they know that they're going to benefit a lot.

3.) Gain Exposure for Your Blog: Use internet marketing techniques that will ensure your blog gains exposure. Some of the internet marketing techniques that you can use include social networking sites search engine optimization ways, viral marketing, pay per click Ads, Google AdWords, etc.

4.) Keep in Touch with Your Audience: You have to do list building. Let the people who are visiting your blog to give you their email addresses willingly. You'll, later on, contact them so that you remind them to visit your blog.

5.) Attract People's Attention: Capture people's attention so that they can keep on visiting your blog. Use headlines that will capture people's attention to read your blog posts. You should also post videos, infographics and include pictures on your blog posts so that they attract people's attention.

6.) Avoid Spelling and Grammar Mistakes: Proofread your articles. Let someone else read your articles before you publish them on your blog. It is to ensure that your articles don't contain spelling and grammar mistakes.

7.) Engage Your Audience: You need to engage your audience. Ask them questions and let them comment on your blog posts. Reply to their comments. This way, your audience will know that you appreciate them and value their opinions. Your audience will trust you, and they'll keep on visiting your blog and also refer people to visit your blog.

8.) Allow Guest Blogging: You should invite experts to publish content on your blog. When you allow experts in your field of specialization to do guest blogging, your blog will gain a good reputation. People will trust it, and this makes your blog to be authoritative.

9.) Quality Products: Selling high-quality products will cause people to visit your blog. Word of mouth will spread much faster about your blog if you're selling a high-quality product that is solving a particular problem that other products haven't been able to resolve.

10.) Buy Traffic: Buying traffic will at least make people know about your blog. Many websites specialize in selling traffic.

The Initial Promotion Strategy

If you are unsure about how to promote your blog, then this is for you. You'll find there are many people out there with blogs, specifically in our industry, but many of them are struggling to get comments and traffic. There are 3 main reasons for this:

❖ They did not take the necessary steps to set up their blog correctly with an Initial Blog Promotion Strategy

❖ They do not have an Ongoing Blog Promotion Strategy

❖ They do not blog consistently.

Here's a step by step on how to promote your blog.

How to Promote Your Blog - A Systematic Approach

❖ Set up a ping list

A ping list is a list of websites that listen for new content on the web. One of your first actions should be to set up your ping list by copying the list of ping services that WordPress provides.

You can find a good list to start with at wordpress.org. Once you copy that list, you paste it in the 'Writing' Section of your WordPress blog settings. On your dashboard go to Settings>Writing and then paste the list in the box titled 'Update Services' and that's it. Now every time you publish a new blog post, each of these services will be notified, and you will start to see traffic to your blog.

❖ Set Up Feedburner

Feedburner provides a way for your users to subscribe to your new blog content. You want people who enjoy your content to come back to your website, and Feedburner gives them a way to subscribe to your blog and be notified whenever you publish new content. It brings you more traffic than if they had to remember to check your blog themselves.

To set up Feedburner go to Feedburner and set up an account. You will have to submit the URL of your feed which, in most cases, will be yourdomain.com/feed.

There are other configuration options to play with but, by submitting to Feedburner, you're pretty much set for your readers to subscribe to your new content.

❖ Install a good SEO Plugin

Several free and paid Plugins help you ensure that each blog post that you publish has specific attributes that make it more appealing to search engines.

Another good option is SEO Pressor, which is a paid option but offers more functionality and automation. These plugins help you ensure your on-page SEO is in order.

❖ Submit your RSS Feed and Blog to Directories

The purpose of submitting your RSS Feed and Blog to directories is the same as maintaining a ping list. You submit your RSS feed and URL to notify various the directories that your blog exists and to keep them updated with your latest posts. These directories are browsed by people who are interested in the type of content you have to offer. The important part of this process is to make sure you submit to the proper category, to match your content with your audience.

A quick search of Google reveals an abundance of blog and RSS directories available to submit your site and your feed. There are both free and paid options. Some places will require a reciprocal link. There are also services that will submit to these directories for you which can be a good deal if your budget allows.

❖ Register for Social Bookmarking Accounts

Social Bookmarking is similar to the bookmarking you do in your internet browser, but instead, you do it publicly on a website. It makes the pages that you bookmark public to the people who share your interests on that site. As a result, people with whom you have common interests can be notified of your new blog posts as you bookmark them. It brings traffic to your site since they share your interests and would probably be interested in what you're reading or bookmarking.

One tip to social bookmarking is not just to bookmark your publications, to not seem self-serving. Be genuine in the articles that you bookmark. You should also bookmark articles from a variety of sources, not just your own. It's also important to reach out and network with people on the social sites so that your built-in audience grows and you get more traffic. Some of the most popular social bookmarking sites are StumbleUpon, Digg, Reddit, Delicious, Diigo, and HubPages. Social bookmarking sites are gradually being overtaken by Facebook and Twitter as the goto sharing sites. However, they are still useful for getting traffic.

❖ Sign up for a Social Bookmarking Automation Tool

Some tools automate submission to the many social bookmarking sites that you will be posting content to. One of the best out there is Onlywire. Using Onlywire cuts down drastically on time required to log in to each Social Bookmarking site and manually post your bookmark. After you've set up your accounts at the different social bookmarking sites, you can pretty much update all of your bookmarks at the push of a button. There is a free version and a paid version of Onlywire. The main difference is the free version is capped at the number of monthly submissions. It's a good idea to start with the free version until you get used to the platform and you have all your accounts set up. Once you begin to promote your blog regularly, you may want to upgrade to a paid version.

5 Most Asked Blog Questions And Answers

Are you considering blogging but want answers to some blog questions before heading to start a blog?

Below are the 5 most common questions being asked about blogging along with answers to them.

Question 1: Is Blogging Safe?

Blogging is safe to a great extent. You have to avoid things that would get you into trouble.

Like if you want to blog for fun, (personal blogging) do not add your personal information (home address, phone numbers, photos of entire family, etc.) to your blog. There have been cases where people who keep own blogs with so much personal information became victims to stickers.

When you blog online, you also want to stay away from copyrighted contents. Do not even use people's content without permission or reference.

Keep these points in mind and blogging would be safe for you.

Blog questions 2: What are some good topics to blog about?

The beauty of online information marketing business whether you are using a blog or a website is that you can write about anything as long as a reasonable number of people come online every day to search for information on the topic. Think deep there is something you know that others would like to hear about.

What are you naturally good at? What do you do for others without thinking that they praise you for? A skill, a hobby, an experience, something you learned or something that annoys you? Think broader.

When you are done with the brainstorming, the next step will be to do complete research on all topics you have chosen at least 3 of them to determine which will be more profitable for you in the long run.

Your research will reveal how many people search for that topic every month. How many people currently write on that topic and how deep the topic is. The related topics under that topic broad enough to form the overall topic of the blog? You don't want to start a blog and get stuck on subjects to write on. It is detailed research required at the beginning. If you choose to jump in without thoroughly researching your topic, it will be like walking blindfolded without knowing where you are going or what awaits you.

Blog Questions 3: How do you earn money blogging?

A single blog can be monetized in several ways! That's the beauty of it. If you put in the hard work, you can get a good result from it.

The way to earn from blogging is through advertisement of different sorts. Some of which you won't know what they mean now, but it's mainly about displaying adverts on your blog related to the content you provide.

The common advertising programs are:

AdSense - pay-per-click advertising program

Text links ad: Advertisements that are formatted as text links

Sell ad space - If you have a good number of visitors to your blog, other bloggers/webmasters will be willing to pay you to display adverts on your blog.

Affiliate marketing - If you blog about network marketing, for example, you can refer your readers to other merchants products related to your topic. If they make a purchase, you get paid a stipulated percentage of the sale.

These are just some of the ways to make money from blogging.

Blog Questions 4: Which is the best blogging website?

The best blogging website is that which meet the needs of your blog.

It wouldn't be exactly right to say this blogging website is better than the other. Whichever meet your blogging goals is the one that is best for you.

So when considering starting a blog, the first question isn't which is the best blogging website. Instead, what is my goal for wanting to start a blog?

What do I hope to achieve from it?

Would the content on the blog be mostly videos, audios or text?

Would there be ads on the blog? If there would, what kind of ads will you use?

These questions and more are what should influence your choice of a blogging website.

You will realize that once you can provide clear answers to these questions, you can then quickly identify the right blogging software for you.

Deciding between WordPress and blogger, if you are considering big-time blogging, you should seriously consider WordPress (the self-hosted version).

But then again blogger will be perfect for you if you want to blog for fun.

Blog Questions 5: How do you get people to start viewing your blog?

Some means to get readers to a new blog are:

Word of mouth - Start by telling friends and family members about your blog

Leave relevant comments on related blogs.

Promote your blog on social networking sites such as Twitter, Facebook, etc.

Bookmark your most important pages on social bookmarking sites like StumbleUpon and delicious. Submit articles to directories.

CHAPTER 9

THE BEST WAYS TO USE KEYWORDS IN YOUR BLOGS

When writing a blog, as with any online marketing technique, learning how to identify and use the right keywords is one of the most crucial things to understand. So if you want to know how to make money blogging with the right keywords, then there are some specific things you should know.

1-Use the Keyword Tools to your Advantage: The keyword research tools available online are an invaluable resource when it comes to the actual process of keyword research and identification. WordTracker and the Google Keyword Tool are probably the top choices to dig on keywords you have in mind and find the most relevant and high traffic keyword phrases. Once you have found the keywords and long-tail keywords that you want to use, this will help you to make sure that your blog will appear at the top of the organic results that look when people do their searches on Google, MSN or Yahoo.

2-Use the Keywords in Your Posts: Another important aspect of how to make money blogging with the right keywords is knowing how to best use your specific keywords within your titles and blog posts. It is where smart strategy comes into play. Be sure to keep your keyword in tact no matter where you use it. Keep it written precisely as your first found it and always try to place it as close to the beginning of your title as possible when using it within a title. Also be sure to place it throughout your posts in a way that sounds natural to your readers without overusing it. You want to optimize your content without ever overdoing it.

3-Training for Keyword Research and Online Marketing: The absolute most important part of your process in learning how to make money blogging with the right keywords, is to be sure to enroll in some Internet marketing and mentoring course that will be able to teach you everything you need to know when it comes to keyword research and online marketing. If you are working on a blog where your goal is to establish a significant following and make a serious income, then the proper training is critical to your success!

Keep in mind that the whole point of writing a blog is for it to be read, and if you mean business about this then you need to be sure you are finding and using the best keywords within your blog to ensure that it gets the highest ranking and views as possible. So the best ways to accomplish this are by using the top keyword research tools, being clever in the usage and making sure to get trained by the best marketing program available so that you can ensure that all of your keyword research and online marketing campaigns will get the best results possible!

How To Automate Your Income

Making money blogging as an affiliate is a great way to start your online career although one that can be frustrating and time-consuming if you take the wrong steps and make the same, classic mistakes. It will talk through some of the best ways to earn a consistent income online and put stability into your money making efforts.

❖ Get a Great Domain Name

When it comes to search engine optimization one of the biggest factors that will give you a head start is to do some keyword research and pick a domain name that you can rank high in the search engines for.

Lots of people pick flashy sounding domain names that don't even give you a clue to what the blog is about. A domain name with a keyword that is easy to place in the top 10 on the search engines, with little serious competition is a substantial factor in getting direct traffic (and sales to your site).

❖ Attract the Right Readers

Blogs are built around content. No secrets there and the content you provide should be offering partial solutions to your reader's problems. The full solution is within the product or reports you're promoting as a newbie affiliate.

The right readers are the ones who are looking to buy and willing to part with some hard earned cash. To make money blogging as an affiliate, it is vital that your target these people. The best way is to make sure the keywords within your post title and content use words like "buy" or "review."

❖ Capture your visitor's details

When you capture your reader's details (name and email address), you build stability into your business. Compare the person looking to make money blogging as an affiliate who has a blog and an email list of 5000 with the affiliate who has a blog. With no email list, you are 100% dependent on getting visitors to your blog each day. Lose a position in the search engines, take time off and stop building traffic and your income will inevitably tail off. Meanwhile, the blogger with the list can email out regularly to promote the same or different products over and over again.

Why Most Bloggers Fail

Do you love to write? At least when it is a topic, we are passionate about. The truth is, it is easier than you think. You can make money blogging about almost any topic imaginable. You are probably wondering why not all bloggers if it was that easy. The fact is, most people don't know how to blog the right way.

There are a few critical factors that can make or break the success of a blog and will determine how much money you can make from it.

1 Critical Element - Blog Title and Domain Name

It makes a huge difference. If no one ever searches for your blog phrase then how will they find you in the search engines? You might have the best content in the world, but if people don't find it, it won't do you much good.

Your domain name also makes a huge difference in how easy it is for people to find you. It is best to have your blog title and domain name match.

2 Critical Element - Your Blog Competition

It is harder to rank well in the search engines for really competitive phrases such as "Weight Loss" or "Golf." You will be much better if you choose a topic that gets a right amount of searches but isn't too competitive.

3 Critical Element - Affiliate Programs

Are there any products you can offer on your blog that can earn you a commission? Some blog topics don't have any way to earn you money. If you choose one that has a lot of great products you can offer, you will make money blogging much easier and faster.

Be Among The Leaders

There is plenty of blogging advice offered on the internet regarding what we will need to do to operate our blog successfully. If you've been thinking about assembling a blog about your business, this blogging advice detailed below is designed specifically for you.

Listed below are the very best strategies an online business blogger can use to seek out visitors. These tips tend to be primarily for new bloggers, those individuals who have a next-to-no market right now and would like to get the process started however if you have been blogging for a while you still might find some useful information in the list below.

It will help if you focus on this particular checklist from top to bottom since every strategy builds upon the previous approach that will help you produce momentum. At some point when you create plenty of energy, you will get what is known as "traction," which usually is a big enough market base (around 500 visitors per day is excellent) which you will no longer need to work so hard in acquiring new visitors. Instead, your current faithful visitors perform the actual work for you by word of mouth marketing.

Be Efficient With These Top Blogging Tips

❖ Create A Minimum Of 5 Main "Pillar" Posts

A pillar post is a mini-seminar style write-up geared to educate your target audience on a specific subject. Usually, they're longer than 500 words with plenty of helpful ideas or advice.

This informative section you're presently reading through might be regarded a pillar post as it is beneficial plus excellent "how-to" training. This brand of writing offers lasting appeal, remains current (it is not information or time centered) while providing actual worth and knowledge. The more pillars you've gotten onto your blog, the more effective.

❖ Create One New Blog Post Each Day

Not each post needs to be a pillar; however, you need to focus on having the five pillars finished all at once while you keep the blog refreshing with new information as well as short brief blog posts.

The biggest thing at this point will be to show your new site visitors that your particular blog will be current on a regular basis so that they feel that if he or she returns down the road, they are going to discover something new most likely. It will cause them to bookmark your blog as well as subscribe to your blog feed.

It's not necessary to create one post each day at all times however it is crucial one does whenever your blog is entirely new. When you receive traction, you will still have to keep your new content coming.

However, your faithful viewers may well be more flexible in the event you lessen the pace to a couple each week instead. The initial few months tend to be crucial therefore the more written content you can generate at the moment the more beneficial.

❖ Create A Lot More Pillar Posts

Anything you choose to do that was previously mentioned will help you get blog visitors. Then again all of the strategies listed here are primarily work when you've got mighty pillars ready. Without having you choose everything previously mentioned you might attract visitors however they will not likely remain or even take the time to return? Strive for one strong pillar post each week, and at the end of this year, you'll have a customer base well over 50 outstanding feature posts designed to work tirelessly so that you can attract increasingly more visitors.

How To Get Readers And Google To Love Your Blog

Do you think Google should help people find articles and posts from the news companies that are suing them over copyright issues? The search giant has no choice but to send traffic to people who are willing to make their content available on generous terms, and to avoid indexing content that others claim copyright to.

It has always been a factor in driving online citizen journalism. It turns out those corporations, nonprofit organizations, religious groups, and political campaigns can also be journalists, and that their journalism can have just as much influence as citizen journalists or media moguls if it's well researched and well produced.

❖ Are you building relation through a network of bloggers?

Building a network is one of the most important aspects of blogging outside of content creation. If you are continually meeting new bloggers and strengthening the relationships that you have made, you will drastically be in a better position for the future. Building a network will help you to learn from others, gain valuable and loyal readers, increase inbound links, increase votes at social media sites, and much more.

❖ Have you set a Goal for your blog?

A goal can vary from one blogger to another but what you must have is a goal for your blog. Usually, a lot of bloggers has long-term goals, like ☐uitting a job and making a living with a blog or getting 5000 subscribers.

Having long-term goals are good but what many bloggers lack is a short-term goal. If you have just started blogging, then it is advised that you have a short-term goal first which will help you to take the necessary steps towards achieving those long-term goals.

For example set monthly goals like how much subscribers, traffic or revenue and then when you achieve these goals, don't give up because you are yet to get towards your long-term goals. Celebrate your success in meeting your short-term goals and keep challenging yourself to achieve the next.

Terms You Need To Know

Precisely what is a Blog? Or RSS? Pinging? Trackbacks? To fully understand a subject, you must learn the 'buzzwords.' Blogs have several special terms which may be new to blogs and blogging. This section briefly lists seven of the terms associated with blogs which should make the beginner more comfortable and able to advance into the blogging world.

1 - Blog, Blogger, Blogging

Blogs have been around on the Internet for a long time. Originally, they were used for product updates and were known as 'weblogs'. The name blog is an abbreviation of the original term.

Simply put, a blog is a journal or diary, where individuals or businesses provide regular, fresh information for readers. Public blogs are available for anyone to read and are usually written for a specific readership audience and are based on a particular topic.

There are many places where you can keep your blog online, and many are free. Favorite free blog hosts include Wordpress.org and Blogger.com, which is owned by Google.

Both of these locations are good because they rank well in Google. That's important because it helps to get your site seen by others.

A Blogger is someone who writes information for their blog.

Blogging is the process of writing the content for a blog.

2 - Template

Both free and paid blog sites allow you to select a template, that makes the blog look appealing to others while establishing it as uniquely yours. The idea is to create an appealing blog with plenty of fresh content containing relevant information.

3 - Niche

A niche is a specialized market, and you need to find a niche that you have an interest in, that others also will find interesting. If you are writing a blog purely to express your own opinions or to let off steam, this is your niche, and may or may not be attractive to others.

Many people would like to make money from their blogs too, by adding an advertising campaign on their site. If this is why you want to create a blog, then your niche needs to have appeal to others. To find a potentially profitable niche requires research.

4 - Post

A post is merely a new entry you add to your blog. Every time you write something and publish it, you are making an original post. Your posts are displayed newest to oldest on your blog site so people can easily see what you have written most recently.

5 - Trackback Links

Trackback links, or trackbacks, advise another blog owner if you've referred to them in a post. Trackbacks are often done automatically in the background by the blog software.

6 - Rss Feeds

RSS feeds are code created by your blog. A feed is a list of your posts and allows readers to subscribe to it. It means that your subscribed readers are notified every time you post something to your blog rather than have to visit often to see if you've posted an update.

7 - Pinging

Pinging sends your most recent blog to blog aggregators which are like blog search engines. These are places that collect blog posts and group them for the interest of others, in a digest form.

Pinging is automatic by some blogs, but you can manually ping your blog yourself. The advantage of pinging is that your blog post is listed on other popular sites and has another way of being found. If you want to ping your posts manually, there is a lot of free software online. Both Ping-O-Matic and Ping FM are very easy to use.

CHAPTER 10

CONNECTING IS THE KEY TO CONNECTION

Blogging is now one of the most popular social past times online today, and people use them to connect with friends, business partners, and followers to let them know what they are currently doing.

Before you start posting you will need to adjust some basic settings to suit your needs. Click the setting tab and add a brief description of your site making sure to use your keywords, blog money making, blogging money, blog for money, earn money blogging, making money blogging, etc., be sure not to overdo it or appear spammy so that it can be read by real people, not just the search engines.

Other settings include the option to make your blog public or private, you will probably set this to the public, but these sets are really up to your preference.

Learn Which Blogging Platform Is Right For You

Numerous blogging services to consider! Well, you've found the right place to discover how to launch a blog. Here's help to decide which blog provider you'll choose.

First, Google's Blogger system is widely used. You can post photos or embed YouTube video, generate links, and all the standard tasks you'd want to do with a blog. You will discover a lot of settings to go through to get it how you want it but all in all a decent platform. You can set up a custom domain, but there are some restrictions.

Second, WordPress is another popular blog platform. WordPress has tons of plug-ins, these are small applications you install that add all sorts of functions to your blog. WordPress is not for newbie bloggers. There are numerous configurations you can get lost in for days.

The user interface is very cluttered. Don't get me wrong, in the right hands, and you can do a lot with WordPress. Just plan on spending a lot of time getting things done. Setting up a custom domain name will cost you extra as that is a paid option. When choosing WordPress, the self-hosted free version is the best way to go if you plan on making money with your blog. All you need is to pay for hosting service and install WordPress.

Third, Empower Network's viral blogging platform. This system has an impressively streamlined user experience making it much faster to get a blog post made. You can start a blog as a beginner and not have to move through a lot of settings. Easily add personalized banners and get started posting. As you learn the ropes of blogging, you can then use their SEO interface for adding keywords and other things to help search engines find your blog. Quick options to set up a custom domain name for each of your blogs.

The significant difference here is ease of use with Empower Network's blog. You can maintain multiple blogs all from the same convenient interface and use sidebar banners.

Another cool feature is media hosting. A lot quicker to upload a video straight to your blog instead of having to upload to YouTube first then embed the video in your blog. Time-saving steps to create a blog so you can center on other important details is what this blog platform is all about. Oh, and a mobile app so it's possible to post anytime from anywhere.

The Ultimate Affiliate Blogger

On your blog, you need to have keyword rich articles about the niche you are talking about. These articles need to give your targeted visitors value. In other words, your articles need to provide solutions to your visitor's problems. You can do this by writing how-to guides and product reviews and posting them on your blog.

At the end of each article, tell your visitors how or where to go to next. If you are marketing a product as an affiliate, you can place your affiliate link at the end of a post telling them to 'click here to find out more.' Remember no selling; let the product page do the selling while you concentrate on giving good advice.

That is all you need to do on your blog. Honestly, it doesn't seem much, but it is the truth. It is the work you need to do away from your blog that is a little more complex. You need to build a web around your blog to get incoming links, which leads to traffic. You can do this in some ways. Posting comments on other blogs are one, writing and posting articles on other websites is another, posting comments on forums, paid advertising. There are far too many to list here, but you get the idea.

Doing these things take time, so don't expect to be making money blogging within your first week. It may take a couple of months of work before you see results. A lot depends on the niche you choose.

When thinking about money blogging, you need to choose a niche carefully. You could go for a competitive niche, but expect a long wait and plenty of work to get high search engine rankings. If you choose a less competitive niche, you may not have as many people searching for you, but you will find it a whole lot easier and quicker to get recognized. Less competitive niches can still bring in plenty of money so are worth going with.

You Must Have Something To Sell

Blogging has become a successful home business for many people. It's an easy business to start because there are few or no startup costs. However, if you want to make money, you must have something to sell on your blog create a "sales" blog.

Although content-heavy blogs on which you sell advertising to make money, these blogs take time before they become profitable, just because you need a lot of content. How much content? Since blogging has become mainstream, and there are many content blogs, it may take at least 500 to 1000 posts on a content blog for profitability.

"Sales" blogs, which sell products or services, can be profitable with as few as ten to 20 blog posts.

So aim for a sales blog, so your blog becomes profitable more quickly.

Before you start blogging, you need a plan. Create your project first, before you create your blog. It's difficult to make money with a blog which hasn't been set up as a money-maker from the start.

Let's look at four easy steps to developing a profitable sales blog.

1. Decide what you'll sell on your blog

To make money, your blog must sell something: a service, or a product. Many bloggers sell affiliate products from their blog.

If you've been blogging for a while, you can sell your blogging services from your blog.

2. Make a list of the products or services which you'll sell

If you're selling as an affiliate, make a list of products you'll sell - reviews of these products will form the basis of your blog articles. Many affiliate bloggers sell lots of products on a single blog. However, it will be more profitable to divide the products you're selling into topics; then create a new blog for each topic. It means that each blog can be more focused, and this will mean more traffic. If you're selling your blogging services, set up the blog to do this. Write articles promoting each service you provide. Essentially, the blog becomes your online portfolio.

3. Start blogging, but keep SALES at the forefront of your mind

Next, you can start writing blog posts. However, plan your posts. Planning is vital for a sales blog. For example, let's say you've created a sales blog to sell affiliate products related to pets.

You've collected ten affiliate products. Plan articles related to those ten products. You can create review-style articles, as well as general content articles with a link to one of your affiliate products.

If you want to get hired as a blogger, then this must be obvious on your blog, and on every post, you write - write several articles promoting each of your services.

4. Promote your blog

Finally, it's time to promote your blog. There are many ways in which you can promote your blog: with classified advertising, Pay Per Click advertising, and article marketing.

How you choose to promote is up to you. However, do remember that you must promote your blog.

Ten Blogging Time Management Tips

Have you started a blog? Millions of blogs have been created, but most bloggers abandon their blogs after a few entries. Of course, these are bloggers who have no blogging goal: they start a blog, but because there's no lure (like money) to encourage them, they stop blogging.

If you'd like to get more organized so that you can blog consistently, here are ten blogging time management tips.

1. Create a file called Blog Ideas

There's nothing more intimidating than a blank computer screen. Create a folder and call it Blog Ideas. Write down any stray thoughts you have about blogging.

Do you have questions about your blogging topic? Your questions can start with: Who, What, How, When, Where and Why - make a note of the questions. In your Blog Ideas file, these are triggers to get you thinking.

Read other blogs. Reading other blogs will stimulate your thinking. Agree with a blogger? Why? Can you expand on a point made in another blog?

Carry a small notebook and jot down ideas which come to you at work. When you're driving, place a digital or microcassette recorder on the passenger seat beside you to record any sudden inspirations.

2. Write five to ten blog posts at a time

Carve out time to blog on the weekends a couple of hours on Saturday afternoon, perhaps. In that time, study your Blog Ideas file, and write a series of posts. These don't have to be polished posts, draft them □uickly. They'll be ready for you to post during the following week.

3. Audio blog

If you're carrying a digital recorder, record some blog posts. It works well for business bloggers. Interview people at your company. Interview with your boss or a couple of your customers.

4. Ask for contributions from other bloggers

Bloggers help bloggers. As you leave comments on others' blogs and get known in the blogosphere, you can ask other bloggers to "guest blog" for you. Ask them to write just one entry, or to write five.

You'll get lots of takers, because blogging for someone else is added exposure for bloggers, and many will take you up on offer. Of course, you'll need to reciprocate and write the occasional entry for others.

5. Out-source - hire a blogger

You can hire bloggers at out-sourcing venues like Elance. It is a good solution for those weeks when your schedule is crammed with other work.

6. Get over perfectionism

When you're blogging, you're not writing a bestseller, nor are you expected to be perfect. If you read any blog, you'll find typos, spelling errors, errors of syntax - part of the charm of reading blogs is their "homemade" appeal. Even if you're writing for a business audience, no one expects you to be perfect.

7. Think about your audience. What challenges do they have?

You're writing for an audience, and that audience has challenges that you can help them to solve.

Write about the problems that your audience faces. Whatever your topic, this ensures that you never run out of material.

8. Research blogging - get up to speed on blogging

A lot of blogging procrastination is just lack of information. Research Blogging. Take a course. You more you know, the more comfortable you'll find blogging.

9. Schedule blogging

Schedule blogging into your day, just as you'd schedule anything else that you have to do.

10. Write product reviews

Whatever your blog's subject area, people are trying to sell products. Review some of the products. Reviews get visitors. Buyers are always looking for product reviews in the search engines, so writing reviews is a way of guaranteeing an audience, and it gives you something to write about.

The Backbone Of Today's Business

There are many reasons why blogging is essential for any business. However, the five goals listed below are the most important ones:

a) Improve visibility

Invite visitors to your website By writing relevant content for your target audience, and you can attract visitors to your website. Marketing of the article in various social networking sites (Facebook, Twitter, and LinkedIn), social bookmarking sites (Reddit, StumbleUpon, and Digg) and forums in which your business is active is key to ensuring visibility of the blog. Content is King, and this applies to a blog as well. The quality of your content will impact visitors. An impactful blog with excellent word power will ensure that the visitors sign up for your blog posts. Blogs create an impression on the visitor, and if your content is helpful, they will share it with others.

b) Cost-effective

Blogging is one of the cost-effective content marketing strategies. Every blog is your asset as it stays as long as your business is active. It is a one-time effort, but the benefits are enormous. If the article is on a general topic which is evergreen (e.g., Benefits of Outsourcing), you will get more benefits as the meaning of these topics are not going to change. On the contrary, if the article is on a specific topic (Tax slab rate for the financial year 2016), the content is relevant to the year 2016 and not beyond that.

c) Branding and Thought Leadership

The quality of content and ideas expressed in your blogs will become the USP (Unique Selling Proposition) for building your brand and promoting you as a 'Thought Leader' in your respective field.

With a good number of blogs on your website and with the help of social networking sites, you will eventually have a list of followers which is only going to increase over the years. These blogs are the ambassadors of your brand and the thoughts/ideas which you share and preach. All this will help you to attract more customers.

d) Engaging your customers

Your blog is the platform where you meet new visitors who are your potential customers and connect with existing customers also. Regular interaction through blogs helps in building a stronger relationship with the customer. Pain points of your customers/ Requirement of your customer which you have highlighted in your blog invoke the interest in your visitor to know more about it, and this will lead to a discussion.

A blog gives you an opportunity to understand your customer requirements better and provide solutions which makes it a win-win situation. Indirectly, it also helps in translating a visitor into a customer who is in need of a similar product or service.

Today's age is an age of engagement, and you have to keep talking to every stakeholder around you to improve your services and identify new business opportunities from your existing customers.

e) Improves SEO

Search engines are always on the lookout for fresh content. There is no better way to keep feeding new content into the web than a blog. Frequent blogs will provide the required fodder to search engines which will identify your website as a credible one. Including keywords, article topics, businesses, product or service which you want to showcase and get defined by search engines in the blog, will serve the purpose of bringing new visitors to the website.

Blogging is an integrated content marketing strategy for every business. It is one of the cost-effective marketing tools for your business.

CHAPTER 11

CONTENT CREATION

Content creation when blogging for cash can be one of the hardest jobs any blogger will face in his or her lifetime. Writing blog posts on a continual basis to maintain the blog's content is hard work. Even the most successful bloggers have had blogging burnout or blogging writer's block from time to time. But done right, regular blogging can be most gratifying and profitable too.

Content creation when blogging for cash need not be complicated or difficult. Being true to your blogging objectives and posting authentic posts will keep away most writer's blocks in general. Keeping up to date with other successful blogs to keep up with your blogging learning will return more tips and ideas for your blog posts. And lastly, keep on writing and posting no matter what and this will eventually pay off in the end.

How Much Content Is Necessary?

You should only ever create as much content as you need to get indexed and ranked for the search terms you are targeting.

Depending on what those terms are you could need anything from some pages or blog posts to a single post.

An example of a single post blog that can get indexed and ranked well and hold that position for years would be one that focuses on a misspelling or some other search word or searches term where there is little or no other competition.

The more competition, the more content you are going to have to add, as well as off-site promotion to ensure that you will rank well, but even in high competition markets lower quantities of good content will always do better than bulk content that is not highly targeted.

Your keyword and market research will determine how much content you need to create to beat the competition and the better that you do that research, the less time you will have to spend on your content and the less content you will need to beat them. It all comes back to the initial preparation before the first amount of content ever gets posted online and that's why it is so important to take the time and not rush your market and keyword research.

It is better to have a tightly focused blog and then to create more blogs in that market which are also tightly focused on other groups of keywords and search terms. Often the content can be duplicated but rewritten to work with the other set of keywords, and this can save you a considerable amount of research time and also give you the ability to link between blogs and therefore boost the ranking of each of those blogs, so they are helping one another.

Where To Get Content From

There are many excellent sources of content on the Internet.

Article directories are one of the best sources because the people for writing content for the article directories have generally done a lot of quality research.

It is a win-win situation because you get the content for free to add to your blog and the people who created the content get links back to their sites and offers.

Don't be concerned about having links from your blog out to other sites. The search engines will see this as a linking to relevant information and if anything they will think that your blog is giving visitors a better experience and this can help you to rank better. You need to have you to offer at the very top of your blog to take advantage of the most critical area of web space and time should that the site visitors take the action that you want them to doing anything else.

Another good source of content is from the latest news items, and you can get these sent to your e-mail address by using Google alerts.

There are very a settings that you can use to get relevant news sent to your e-mail address and once you understand that you can sort through it and post what you choose for your blog.

It is an easy clip way of updating your blog with new content on a daily basis mainly if you use the ability to post via e-mail to Blogger.

It only takes minutes a day to look through the e-mails that come to you too and then forward them on to your Blogger blog.

In WordPress, you will need to copy and paste the content into your blog.

It takes a little longer, but it is still a small task to do each day and a great way to get good content for free.

Points To Write An Awesome Blog Post

In today's time, when thousands of blog posts are updated on a daily basis, it is challenging to create a niche for a new blog. If you are a novice in the realm of blogging and looking for some tips to write a great post, you are in the right place. This has been written to provide readers with eight basics points that every novice blogger must know to get success in the blogging world.

In simpler words, blogging is just like a personal diary. You share your thoughts on your blog as you write a diary. The main difference is that your blog is not personal. So, whatever you write on your blog will be shared with your readers. The main idea behind blogging is sharing knowledge with others. If you are new to blogging, you should follow eight basic points, which are as follow:

1. You should always blog about what you know that best. Don't follow what most of the readers are reading. You should always write about the things you understand well. Only then, you can create a niche for your blog.

2. You should still use plain English. Try to avoid colloquial language. Blogging is all about merely explaining complex things.

3. Write an intriguing title for your blog post. The title of your blog post should not be more than 8-9 words. The title should be self-explanatory and straightforward so that readers can get an idea about what they will read.

4. You should try to use subheadings and bullet points as much as possible. This will make your blog post easy to read.

5. If you are using facts and figures in your blog post, make sure you use them correctly. You will lose credibility as a blogger if readers find mistakes in your blog post.

7. You should proofread your blog twice. No one likes to read the lousy writing.

8. Include at least 2-3 images in your blog post. A blog post with images attracts more visitors.

You should read leading blogs to get an idea of how to write a blog post.

Advice For Regenerating Your Blog

Blogging is well known as a brilliant way to regularly add new content, promote your business and develop more leads. However, we are still hearing instances where clients start a blog, enjoy success in the beginning then a few months down the line, things go quiet and followers, comments and shares seem to be a thing of the past. Why is this?

We've had a look at some client case studies and have come up with some methods you can employ to keep your blog active and your followers interested.

Firstly, don't relax! So you've built your blog, and have developed a healthy following.

Don't just keep posting blindly in the hope they will stay and continue to follow you. Blog readers are a fickle bunch. If the content is not continually exciting and relevant, readers can quickly become bored. To own a successful blog you need to persevere, and with dedication and hard work, keep at it on a regular basis.

❖ Keep your blog looking fresh

If you want your followers to visit your blog, say once a week; give them something new and exciting to look at. A blog which never changes always looks the same, and only posts the same type of boring article will very quickly lose followers.

❖ Irregular posting is lazy

Don't be a lazy blogger. Forgetting to post or leaving it for an extra few days is the worst thing you can do. A blog is a powerful way to build a real connection with your readers and to present yourself to them. With regular posts, you can create your reputation in their minds and your relationship with them. Ignore them, and they'll go off and find someone more interesting to read. Make a posting on your blog a regular habit.

Play around with it and figure out what your optimum post level per week is, based upon responses and comments. Some of our bloggers post on a daily basis, the minimum for a successful blog seems to be three blogs per week.

Posting regularly will open up more opportunities for two-way communication with your followers too. Think of it this way; if you talk to them, they'll talk to you. If you ignore them, why should they hang around?

❖ Too many adverts are off-putting

Advertising on a blog is a way many bloggers choose to boost their income. There's no doubt it can work but be careful. Bombarding your readers with pop-up adverts and distracting PPC will put them off. The most popular blogs, we have found, are those who are clean, advert free, or if they do have adverts, they are carefully placed and not obtrusive in any way. The reader's enjoyment of the blog remains the focus.

Adverts which complement the content of your blog are powerful and can generate you a good income. However, at the other end of the spectrum, going nuts and overloading your page with poorly designed adverts, all flashing and clashing against each other, and drowning out your own brand identity is a fatal error. Don't let your quality content get lost in a sea of other people's cheap advertising.

It's best to stick to no more than three adverts per page. Two good quality adverts, well placed and complimentary to your blog will work much better for all concerned. Think about your readers with courtesy. What do you like to see when you read a blog, the article or a page full of adverts?

❖ Get dressed up and look professional

On or offline, appearances are so important. Make sure your blog is well dressed at all times. The design, layout, and theme of your website are all essential ways of portraying your brand image successfully to readers. The content should reflect you that's words, pictures and design the whole package. Your blog should look attractive, professional and fresh. Do a little customer research. Ask for feedback and listen to the comments you receive. Have a look at other favorite blogs too. Look at how they are designed to suit their particular subject area or industry.

Your choice of background color, font and layout can make a massive difference to how your blog is perceived and whether viewers regard YOU as a professional or an amateur. If you have the budget to employ a professional to help you design your blog, we strongly recommend it.

If you are building it yourself, then take the time to read about blogs, research other blogs and carefully plan and design your blog don't be tempted to hash something together quickly. Blogs that look home-made or sloppy never enjoy good results regarding popularity amongst followers. Try different styles out with a sample group of readers. Ask questions of other successful bloggers. Put the hard work in.

From day one, your blog is an online representative of you and your professional standing. Don't let yourself down.

Blogging Your Way To The Higher End

If you want to blog your way to the higher end, that means you are ready to make money. A good product does not sell itself. You have to make the availability of the product known. It calls for advert placement on your site. There are a lot of companies that are willing and ready to place adverts on your blog. The adverts have to relate to your blog title and keywords.

These adverts are what generate money for you as a blogger. For instance, you can get adverts from any of the sites by cutting and pasting their HTML code in your site. It's as simple as registering with any of them, and after the approval, your HTML code will be given to you, and you cut and paste. Another perfect way of monetizing your blog is by registering and participating in affiliate programmes. Place the banners for the programmes you want to promote in your site, and you are paid anytime somebody registers through your blog site.

To place banner codes, go to your dashboard, click on add gadget, then choose HTML in the options available and paste your code. Another significant thing to do is to make sure that your blog settings are optimized to give access to search engines and always remember to enable your show backlinks.

CHAPTER 12

STEPS TO FINANCIAL FREEDOM

To Help You Pay Your Bills And More

Imagine what life would be like if you make money blogging. A moneymaking blog will pave the way to creating greater financial freedom as well as generate a great deal of excitement in your life. With a shortage of jobs on the market these days, blogging is one of the easiest ways to get started making a genuine income online. Here are 6 good reasons to blog for profit.

*Many people blog for personal fun and enjoyment, why not use blogging as a business. With the economy presently in the dumps, it is an excellent means to earn some extra cash to help with the car payment, keep the creditors happy, pay the cell phone bill or just plain helping to make ends meet.

*Having a business blog doesn't mean you have to be an excellent writer to make money blogging. All you need is to have good ideas about a topic and write those ideas into your blog. Keep on writing as the more you write, the easier it will get for you.

*Besides, blogs are just websites, but unlike standard websites, they are much easier to set up and update. Blog websites use simple programs, like a word processor program. If you can write an email, then you have the skills to start blogging for profit. Another great thing is that your workplace is flexible. All you need is a laptop and an internet connection, and you can blog anywhere.

*A business blog can be the solid base for both an online and offline business. It's a great marketing tool to attract a large group of customers to your online presence or send them flocking to your offline store.

*No matter what your background or where you are from, anyone can start to make money blogging. While you won't get rich overnight, blogging is something anyone can become good at and in a few weeks be able to blog for profit.

Resources That Are Worth Your Time

Now is the time to reassess your internet marketing strategies and get rid of anything that no longer works. Many are wondering today whether a blog is worth the time that you put into it. Whether you have a blog already or you are considering starting one shortly, this is a question that you need to be answered as soon as possible.

❖ Blogging Remains Relevant

Perhaps your current blog is lacking in traffic, or you are just getting started and worried it is too late. It is not the case.

You can rest easy if you are worried that blogging these days is a waste of time. It will continue to work for you now and for a long time to come. Therefore, if you are thinking about starting a blog our increasing your efforts on your existing one, it is wise to keep it as an integral part of your marketing strategy.

❖ Increased Inbound Links

Statistics show that companies who have blogs acquire 97% more inbound links. It is no secret that incoming links increase the credibility of your website with search engines. When other reliable sites link to your site, you are deemed trustworthy via association. Your site will rank higher, and you will be viewed as an authority within your industry.

Besides, the visitors to those other sites will follow the links to your site, leading to more traffic for you. As long as your blog content is worthwhile, you can expect a drastic increase in prospects for your business.

❖ Declining Human Contact

Experts predict that within the next four years, 85% of customer relationships will not be managed with human interaction. With developments in technology continuing to rise, the customer is going to use that technology rather than speak to a human.

It means that you can expect upfront contact to continue to decrease in the coming years. Customers are going to be doing research on their own and making assessments before making any calls. With a popular blog filled with quality content, you will stand out as the best company for the job.

❖ Trusted Resource

Today, blogs are considered to be the most trustworthy source for precise information on the internet. Blogs naturally feel intimate, regardless of whether they are business or personal.

With the development and delivery of consistent quality content, your blog will quickly become the go-to resource for trusted content within your particular industry. Besides, by responding to customer questions and comments, you highlight a commitment to assisting your readers in finding the information they require.

When You Are Not Getting the Desired Results from Your Blog

In some cases, you may already have a blog, but are not reaping the desired benefits. The reason for this is likely that you are not making blogging a big enough priority in your marketing efforts. To obtain the results that you want, you have to be consistent and the content that your product has to be of the highest quality on topics that will interest your target audience. It is where you are going to find true value.

It is a fact that maintaining a blog will take a considerable amount of time. However, by putting in the effort and making your blog a top priority, you will enjoy a greater return on your investment than marketers who do not blog.

In contrast, if your posts have been consistent and your content is great, then you should dig deeper. The problem may lie with the calls-to-action at the end of your blog posts. While your main priority should be to provide the reader with excellent content, you need to prompt them to take action once they have read the post.

Discover The Pros And Cons Of Blogging

A lot of people have already discovered the benefits of having a blog. Others, however, are still undecided about it. Blogs are used for different reasons. Some use it as a marketing strategy; to establish themselves as an expert, build trust with potential customers, and then redirect them to a website where the reader can buy their products. Others use it either as an online diary or as a means of making money. In this post, are the pros and cons of having a blog.

❖ Pros

* Marketing - As said above, a blog is a perfect way to market your product

* Possible income - If you can get enough visitors to your blog, and enough subscriptions to your RSS feed, companies will want to advertise on your blog. Alternatively, you can get paid commission by 'affiliate' selling, where you mention a product sold by someone else, and for anyone who that product, and was directed from your site, you earn commission.

* Traffic from search engines - Search engines regularly scan blogs and add them to their search listings. The more pages your blog has, and the more relevant it is to the search term, the higher up your link will appear. It is good because you will get more visitors each day, which means more people to click your link; either to your products, or someone else's.

* Feedback - A blog is a great way to get some feedback about your product. Make sure you enable the comments though. Otherwise, you won't get any!

* Reputation - As long as you don't have any silly spelling or grammar mistakes, your blog will help build not only your company's reputation, but also it's brand awareness as well.

* Free - Most blogs are free. Others, however, cost money, but these usually have better features and stats analytics.

Cons

* Reputation - Mainly, this is a pro, because most of the time a blog will improve your company's reputation. As said above, however, any mistakes, speaking out of term, or giving incorrect information can seriously tarnish your reputation. It takes years to build a reputation, and seconds to destroy it.

* Time - While blogging is mainly free, you may see it as free marketing. It's not. Ever heard the phrase 'Time is money'? Silly question, of course, you have! A blog takes a lot of time to maintain, and if you fail to support it, it could harm your reputation.

* Legal - Beware of this one. If you offer advice to your readers, make sure you include a disclaimer. If one of your readers decides to take you up on your advice, and it all goes wrong for them, chances are it will also go wrong for you, as they will either spam your blog with negative comments or in the worst case scenario, commence legal action against you.

Excellent Tips For All Your Blogging Needs

If you are trying to make your online business a success, then you should seriously consider blogging as a powerful tool to aid you in generating traffic to your Website. If you set up and maintain your blog, then it can you get huge returns with little very little investment.

Some great tips to get you started building your blog and aid you in maintaining it, are listed below:

1. In this case, the old saying, "Less is more" can certainly be true. Just like sitting through a seminar that goes on and on, so is reading through a lot of wordy material. Get to the point and put your ideas on a blog without writing too much.

2. Write about one plan at a time. It is the best way to get the interest of your audience and keep it is to stick to one point at a time. If you begin to jump from one subject to the next, you will lose your reader's interest very quickly.

3. Remember, just because you know a lot about a topic, doesn't mean everyone else does. State your ideas in an unambiguous format, so even a first-grader could understand it.

4. Make a connection with your audience by maintaining an informal approach that allows the readers to read your blog and feel as if they're talking to you.

5. Proofread your work very carefully. No one wants to see misspelled words or bad grammar when they're trying to educate themselves about something. It seems to defeat the purpose.

6. Be positive. We all need some encouragement in this day and age, where gas is $4 a gallon and so is milk, and the media are continually debating if we're in a recession or not. Keep your blogs positive and uplifting, and it will

affect your reader.

Structuring Your Blog Properly With SEO

SEO, or search engine optimization, is an essential component of your blogs ability to rank well. SEO is a complex topic that can be frustrating for a beginning marketer, which is one reason why an estimated 95% of people fail at online marketing.

For SEO to be active on your website, you should make sure your blog is properly structured. Your blog will thrive better if it's set up correctly. Continually structuring and posting content, not having enough links or too many links at one time, and other factors can destroy your chances in ranking in the search engines. This is why it's so important to structure your blog to make search-engine optimization easier properly.

1.) Structure your blog

The first step to structuring your blog performing keyword research. Use keyword research to discover what keywords rank best in the search engines. Go to Google and search for 'Google AdWords' or 'keyword research tool.' Type in a keyword or set of keywords that are related to your niche and see how many search results come up for each month. You want to use keywords that get at least 100,000 searches a month, and that preferably have low or medium competition. When first starting out, it's usually best to rank for low to medium competition keywords if you want better chances of ranking higher.

Select around 7 to 15 keywords and copy them to your notepad. You will be using these for your keywords or 'tags' when posting on your blog. You want to sprinkle the keywords you're trying to rank for throughout all of your blog posts. Putting too many keywords in your post could be considered as spam, so you may want to limit the number of keywords you use. Below are a few basic SEO tips you can apply to your blog.

1.) Make sure to use your target keyword in your blog title.

2.) Use one other similar keyword

3.) Use target keywords in Meta tags

4.) Use target keyword in header tag 1, but only one time.

An example of an h2 tag Looks like this

As you could probably guess, the tag pattern continues like this:

The H2 tag Looks like this

The H3 tag Looks like this

and so on...

5.) Use your keyword as the alt text in one or more images on your blog

6.) Use about 5 to 7 generic keywords in your post. These can be keywords that are similar to the one you are already ranking for. So for example, say your target keyword is 'make money online.'

Some generic keywords you could use are 'how to make money online,' 'make money online free,' 'make money free,' 'how to make money free,' free ways to make money,' etc. Just make sure your generic keywords are ranking high as well.

7.) Make videos that teach people how to do something or try writing some of your articles into a Powerpoint layout. You can record your voice reading the content of the presentation to give your visitors a better idea of who you are.

8.) Link your blog to other sites on the internet. Free and paid backlinking is a big, yet complex part of SEO that contributes traffic to your blog.

After setting up your content in the correct and writing your blog posts all in the proper structure, you should add videos, images, polls, comment areas, games, just anything that makes your blog stand out and beneficial to the reader. Make your blog stand out with a variety of blog posts that contain valuable information and videos or images. Add social media buttons to your blog as today many people love to share articles, blog posts, and videos they liked.

Share your content on social media websites, post on guest blogs, or post links to your content in forums and other blogs that are related to your niche. Promoting your blog and networking with others in your niche are two of the most important skills you should have in internet marketing. This is why you should use social media to establish a presence and promote your content.

2.) Promote your blog with social media

Creating profiles on several different social media websites is the best way to develop a social presence, which will eventually help with your blog's traffic.

Listing information about yourself and including a picture or video is a great way to gain the trust of visitors that come to your website. People like to see who's posts they are reading and fell more connected to authors they can relate to.

Here are some social media sites that you should get accounts with to help establish your online presence.

1.) Facebook

2.) Linkedin

3.) Twitter

4.) Pinterest

5. Instagram

6.) Digg

7.) Facebook group or fan page

Creating a Facebook group or Fanpage can help build a fan base and direct visitors to your blog. Fan pages have the potential to bring in tons of traffic to your website and that you can present future offers to.

Promotion and visitors= backlinks

You can think of backlinks as votes. The more backlinks your blog has, the higher your ranking is going to be. So what exactly are backlinks?

Backlinks are links posted on other web pages that contain your link. These are a great way to get traffic and there are are many ways to get backlinks.

Backlinks can be manually posted in blog comment areas, forums, and other pages that have similar content to yours. There are backlinking tools that will distribute hundreds of backlinks for you at a time. There is some excellent software for this such as Backlink Energizer or many other backlink building software, however these cost around fifty to a hundred bucks. Both are well worth the investment, but if you don't have the money, then manual link posting may be the way to go.

ABOUT THE AUTHOR

Paul D. Kings is a Software Engineer, Father, husband, and self-published author. He likes to write about selling and making money online. Paul has been selling on eBay and Amazon since 2007.

www.ingramcontent.com/pod-product-compliance
Lightning Source LLC
Chambersburg PA
CBHW031244050326
40690CB00007B/949